Criminology: A Very Short Introduction

T0054843

VERY SHORT INTRODUCTIONS are for anyone wanting a stimulating and accessible way into a new subject. They are written by experts, and have been translated into more than 45 different languages.

The series began in 1995, and now covers a wide variety of topics in every discipline. The VSI library currently contains over 550 volumes—a Very Short Introduction to everything from Psychology and Philosophy of Science to American History and Relativity—and continues to grow in every subject area.

Very Short Introductions available now:

Tim Newburn

CRIMINOLOGY

A Very Short Introduction

OXFORD
UNIVERSITY PRESS

Great Clarendon Street, Oxford, OX2 6DP,
United Kingdom

Oxford University Press is a department of the University of Oxford.
It furthers the University's objective of excellence in research, scholarship,
and education by publishing worldwide. Oxford is a registered trade mark of
Oxford University Press in the UK and in certain other countries

© Tim Newburn 2018

The moral rights of the author have been asserted

First edition published in 2018

Published in the United States of America by Oxford University Press
198 Madison Avenue, New York, NY 10016, United States of America

British Library Cataloguing in Publication Data
Data available

Library of Congress Control Number: 2017962184

ISBN 978-0-19-964325-7

Printed and bound by
CPI Group (UK) Ltd, Croydon, CR0 4YY

Links to third party websites are provided by Oxford in good faith and
for information only. Oxford disclaims any responsibility for the materials
contained in any third party website referenced in this work.

Contents

Acknowledgements

As ever, I have accumulated many debts in the writing of this book. Much of it has been tested through teaching, and subsequently revised and improved. I had initially planned that this book would be written collaboratively with several groups of my students. Although it did not quite come to fruition in the way I hoped, I nevertheless owe a great deal to my SA105 Crime & Society (2015/16) and SA403 Criminal Justice Policy (2015/16 and 2016/17) classes. I hope they'll recognize a little bit of themselves in this volume. My thanks also to Jenny Nugee and Andrea Keegan, my editors at OUP, who have been unfailingly patient and supportive, and to Joy Mellor for her careful work on the final text.

A number of friends and colleagues took time out of their already overly busy lives to comment on full drafts of this book and I'm enormously grateful to Leo Cheliotis, George Mair, Coretta Phillips, Robert Reiner, and Paul Rock for their generous help. In this regard, I owe very particular thanks to David Garland, whose kind but very rigorous reading of the initial draft helped shape and significantly improve the final version while giving me confidence that I was travelling in broadly the right direction. I would also like to acknowledge, with gratitude, the advice or support of the following colleagues: Jennifer Brown, David Downes, Trevor Jones, Insa Koch, Niki Lacey, Alyce McGovern,

Jill Peay, Peter Ramsay, Meredith Rossner, Michael Tonry, Tank Waddington, Andy Ward, and Don Weatherburn.

Finally, and as always, my greatest debt is to my family, and most particularly and in innumerable ways (up to and including the shape of the final paragraph of this book), to my wife Mary. Though it is a while ago now, it was seeing my children as teenagers read, enjoy, and learn from *Very Short Introductions* that convinced me to take on this project. This book is dedicated to Gavin, Robin, Lewis, and Owen, and to my grandchildren, Georgia, Freya, and Ethan.

List of illustrations

The publisher and the author apologize for any errors or ommissions in the above list. If contacted they will be pleased to rectify these at the earliest opportunity.

Chapter 1
Introducing criminology

In one of his few observations about crime, and in this case slightly tongue in cheek, Karl Marx said, 'A philosopher produces ideas, a poet poems, a clergyman sermons, a professor compendia and so on. A criminal produces crimes.' His point was that while we may be used to thinking of crime in moral terms, as something to be avoided or prevented, it can also be seen as a branch of production. 'Would locks ever have reached their present degree of excellence had there been no thieves?', he asked. That we see some acts as crimes, and the people who commit these things as criminals, gives rise to a wide variety of occupations and professions: from police, prison, and probation officers, to court officials and judges, and, of course, criminologists. That so many 'benefit' from crime—including people like me—is a reminder to us, if we need it, that the business of criminology is not a neutral one.

In fact, criminology is a deeply *political* enterprise. It has something to study only because there are social rules, such rules are occasionally broken, and some of those that break them are punished. But only *some*. While arguably even the most powerful are constrained by the law, the theft, damage, and destruction done by those in such positions is rarely punished. Indeed, often it is not even called 'crime'. So, we need to think carefully about why certain things are defined as criminal, and who has the power to make such decisions. We will return to this in Chapter 2.

The eminent American scholar, Edwin Sutherland, writing over three-quarters of a century ago, observed that criminology is the body of knowledge regarding crime as a social phenomenon that includes within its scope the process of making laws, of breaking laws, and of reacting towards the breaking of laws. Though there are a variety of issues that one can take with this definition—not least as a consequence of the observation earlier about the behaviour of the powerful—it still serves as a helpful introduction to what the subject is about.

Criminology has its origins in the late 18th century and began, it has been argued, as a series of cottage industries, each the product of small groups of people developing an interest in explanations for crime alongside their main occupations such as running asylums or collecting statistics on prisons or court proceedings. Such work carried on largely independently rather than as any form of collective enterprise until the late 19th to early 20th century. Furthermore, few if any of these scholars would have referred to themselves as 'criminologists'. At this point, such work would most likely have been labelled anthropology, jurisprudence, political economy, psychiatry, phrenology, science of police, or statistics.

Slowly over the course of the 20th century this thing we now recognize as 'criminology' gradually formed and solidified. Its constitutive disciplines include (at least) sociology, history, psychology, law, and statistics. Despite its growing profile as a subject of study with textbooks, degrees, university departments, academic journals, annual conferences, prizes, and honours, criminology is still best conceived as a subject or field of study, rather than as a discipline itself. That is to say, as David Garland has put it, criminology 'has no distinct theoretical object and no distinct method of inquiry of its own'. It draws on the theories and methods of other disciplines and, as such, is best thought of as a 'rendezvous subject'—a place where people from differing academic perspectives come together.

One consequence of this is that there is little agreement as to how criminology should be seen and done. So, what is a criminologist? When I'm asked what I do, I'm never sure what kind of response saying 'criminologist' will produce. Some people have been known to greet this news with long diatribes about the woeful state of the criminal justice system and why we need to lock people up and throw away the key. Others will respond with an excited reaction, wanting to know what it is like to set about catching criminals. Still others, much influenced by the CSI franchise of TV programmes, will ask something about the latest techniques for criminal profiling and, of course, about serial killers.

At the risk of losing readers on page 3, now is the time to admit that these assumptions about criminology are, at best, a little wide of the mark. Most of my colleagues and I are not involved—certainly in any day-to-day way—in investigating crime. Although there are forensic specialists out there, CSI-style work generally does not feature in mainstream criminology. And while my job has its occasional excitements, that is much more to do with seeing my students succeed than it is the thrill of chasing serial killers.

In the hope that you are still with me at this point, a few words now about what this book is actually about. My aim is to give you an insight into the nature of criminology; to raise some of the more important questions confronting criminology; to puncture certain myths about crime and criminals; and to use some of the latest research to give a sense of what we know about crime and criminality—and, therefore of course, also of what we still can't claim to know.

We will begin by looking in some detail at one of the core concerns of criminology: *crime*. A superficially simple idea, we will quickly come to see that there is more to it—much, much more—than meets the eye. In fact, this part of the subject of criminology is highly problematic and first and foremost we must learn to treat it with considerable caution. With such caution in mind we will then focus on two important questions. First, who commits crime; and, second, what have been the major trends in crime in recent decades? Are our societies becoming more or less crime-prone, and how might we explain such trends?

Having looked at the nature of crime and criminality, together with trends in crime, we will turn our attention to the matter of how we respond to, and deal with, crime. We will learn a little about the limits of the formal criminal justice system (police, courts, prisons, and so on), and think a little about the role of more informal sources of social control such as families, schools, and neighbourhoods. Linked with this, and last of all, we will look at what is known about crime prevention: that burgeoning body of activity that focuses on how to make crime less easy or less attractive to commit.

In a 500-page book entitled *What is Criminology?* published a few years ago, over thirty authors examined various aspects of contemporary criminology. Their concerns varied from the nature of criminology, how it should be done, through to its purpose and its impact. The image of criminology that emerges from the volume is of a highly variegated subject, full of critical self-examination, containing individuals with widely differing perspectives and priorities. That so many differences and disagreements exist is, in my view, more a source of strength than it is of weakness. It is indicative of a subject rich in possibilities and one, I will hope to persuade you, full of exciting and important questions.

Chapter 2
What is crime?

For some critical scholars the most problematic thing about criminology is its focus on *crime*. Why is this a problem you might well ask? The answer is worth exploring in some detail for not only will it improve our understanding of the subject matter of criminology, it will make us ask the important question: what is the point of *criminology*? Indeed, in thinking about this some have argued that we should simply abandon the idea of criminology altogether and instead focus our attentions on a variety of other matters, such as deviance of all kinds, some of which might fit into a traditional conception of criminology, and some which undoubtedly go quite a way beyond.

First of all, how might we define crime? What does the dictionary say? The *Oxford English Dictionary* defines it variously as:

1. An evil or injurious act; an offence, a sin; esp. of a grave character
2. An act or omission constituting an offence (usually a grave one) against an individual or the state and punishable by law

Perhaps the most straightforward way, as in the second dictionary definition above, is to view *crime* as a violation of the criminal law. In the abstract, then, from this viewpoint those matters we call crimes are simply the things we identify via the criminal law as acts that potentially result in the imposition of a penalty. But law and morality intersect. In the criminal law a distinction has often been drawn between offences referred to using the Latin term *mala in se*, being offences considered wrong in themselves, and those referred to as *mala prohibita*, or offences that are wrong because they are prohibited. In short, there are some behaviours—including murder, rape, robbery, and theft—that are prohibited, and are considered *wrong*, almost everywhere, and a broader range of offences that may vary considerably jurisdiction by jurisdiction and over time.

There are, of course, also civil matters that can result in penalties being imposed—in England, for example, there is a wide array of offences relating to the transport and employment of immigrants—but these are not all *crimes*. A narrow criminal-law-based approach to criminology would be extraordinarily restrictive. Looking at crime this way would also lead us to ignore some very important social, political, and philosophical questions, not the least of which is, why are some things subject to criminal penalties and others are not? We will explore this later in relation to 'white collar' illegalities. Finally, and relatedly, the strict interpretation takes the application of the criminal law at face value. It doesn't ask, for example, how the criminal law is enforced and why it is enforced in the ways it is. The way in which the law is applied has very real consequences for individuals and groups, and it may also affect, in turn, the way we understand and think about crime. So, the fact that some crimes are much more regularly punished than others—benefits fraud and theft from shops versus illegal downloading from the Internet for example—may both influence the way in which we think about these acts (is one worse than the other?) and even influence people's likelihood of engaging in such acts.

What if we extend our gaze, as some have urged we should do, and take our focus as being violations of moral and social, rather than simply legal, codes? In many respects this is the approach taken by those who describe themselves as 'sociologists of deviance', perhaps the dominant criminological approach in the 1960s and 1970s, and one which continues to exert considerable influence. This at least allows the criminologist to examine forms of behaviour that might be considered non-conformist or deviant, even if not always legally criminal. If our concern is with social order and social control then surely we don't want to be restricted simply to what legislators have defined as criminal. Let us take an example: graffiti.

Associated especially with a variety of youth subcultural styles, and with hip hop in particular, graffiti has become an urban art form/social problem (take your pick) of considerable importance and visibility in recent decades. Tracing its modern origins is tricky, but certainly it became a popular and visible activity in New York City in the 1970s and 1980s. Initially undertaken anonymously, gradually those involved began to identify themselves via 'tags', and as graffiti became more elaborate and stylized, anonymity became increasingly problematic. Graffiti, for many, was now a public display and even an art form, and a number of practitioners slowly became famous. The painter Jean-Michel Basquiat began as a graffiti artist with the tag 'SAMO©'. In 2010, *Time* magazine selected the British street artist 'Banksy' as one of its top hundred most influential people. In some senses graffiti had entered the mainstream. Nevertheless, despite such well-known public figures and their pricy art, much graffiti was still viewed as nothing but a blight, disfiguring public transport and private property. How, then, should it be understood? Is it crime/criminal? Should it be the focus of study for the criminologist? The answer to this latter question is a fairly definitive 'yes'. And it is 'yes' for several reasons.

The first and perhaps most obvious reason lies in the answer to the first question: that, yes, under some circumstances graffiti is something that is treated as criminal. Indeed, the response of authorities to graffiti can tell us much about the social control of public space and public property, and about perceptions of youth and youthful activity. Second, for some criminologists there are interesting questions raised by the social reaction to graffiti in terms of crime prevention techniques and their impact, and we will revisit this in greater detail in Chapter 8. But there is another reason why graffiti might be thought to be a pertinent topic for criminology: it helps us reflect on the boundaries of conduct and, more particularly, what we consider to be 'deviant' or in some way 'problematic'. By focusing on the lives of those engaged in such activities we confront some of the challenges to contemporary social order—and, possibly, are invited to think afresh about different ways in which our social order, our society, might be arranged.

Relativity

The next issue we need to confront is the historical and cultural relativity of much crime. Put more straightforwardly, we need to acknowledge that not everything that was once criminal remains so, and vice versa, and not everything considered criminal in one place is treated as criminal everywhere else. As I have implied, there are three main ways in which we can think about the *relativity* of crime, by considering: those things that used to be illegal but are no longer; matters which were once quite freely done but are now subject to legal restriction; and, finally, those things that are legal in some jurisdictions but illegal in others.

There are, naturally, a great many examples of things that were once illegal but have more recently become permissible. In both the United States and the United Kingdom, for example, abortion was once a criminal offence. After a lengthy political campaign in the UK, the Abortion Act 1967 made the termination of pregnancy legal under specific circumstances. Similarly, the landmark Supreme Court decision in the US in 1973, known as *Roe v. Wade*, ruled that the right to privacy under the 14th Amendment included a woman's right to abortion. How secure are these legislative changes? Reasonably so, it would appear in the UK, though there are challenges, but much less so in the US where the judgement has always been contentious and where critics have more recently been emboldened by the election of President Trump and his promise to appoint conservative Supreme Court justices. The legalization of homosexuality is another example of change in this direction. The Sexual Offences Act 1967 decriminalized homosexual acts in private between adult males (at that time over the age of 21) in the UK. In the US, since a Supreme Court ruling in 2003, all sexual activity between consenting adults of the same sex has been deemed legal. Prior to that there was very considerable local variation between states.

A third example of such change would be changes in the legal status of *miscegenation* or, more particularly, the existence and later repeal of laws banning marriages between people considered to be of different races. In South Africa, under the apartheid regime, so-called 'mixed marriages' were outlawed between 1949 and 1985. There were laws prohibiting marriages between white and black people in the US from the late 17th century. A majority of states continued to enforce such laws up until the Second World War. Significant change eventually came as a result of a case brought by the wonderfully named Mildred and Richard Loving, the focus of the 2016 Hollywood film (simply called *Loving*). Legally married in Washington, DC, in 1958, the Lovings were subsequently arrested some weeks later in Virginia where their marriage wasn't recognized. They pleaded guilty to 'cohabiting as man and wife, against the peace and dignity of the Commonwealth' and were sentenced to one year in prison, suspended on condition they left the state. Some years later, after Mildred Loving had written to the Attorney General, Robert Kennedy, a case was filed on her behalf by the American Civil Liberties Union. After a period of almost three years their case reached the Supreme Court which, in June 1967 eventually ruled in the Loving's favour. Nevertheless, anti-miscegenation laws remained on the books (even if unenforceable) in several states, with Alabama becoming the last state to finally remove all mention of anti-miscegenation from its constitution in 2000.

Termination of pregnancy, consensual sex between men, and marriage between people of different 'races' are all clear reminders that many of the things that are now legal were very much treated as *crimes* until very recently. What, then, of changes in the other direction: matters once freely undertaken but now subject to criminal sanction? Let me offer three very different examples. A first and perhaps obvious one concerns the criminalization of particular substances—something which has largely been undertaken during the course of the 20th century. Many readers will be familiar with the fictional detective, Sherlock Holmes, and his predilection for cocaine, a substance that allowed him to escape from the 'dull routine of existence'. It is quite possible that Arthur Conan Doyle, Holmes' creator, was an opium user, certainly Charles Dickens was known to have smoked it. Opium was freely accessible in England until the late 1860s, and there was little moral condemnation of such activities during the Victorian era, with serious attempts at control only beginning in the early 20th century. The United States made the manufacture, importation, and possession of heroin illegal in the mid-1920s, but it was not until mid-century that the worldwide movement to ban heroin was fully underway. Most developed countries now have an extensive and complex series of prohibitions relating to a range of substances, and the so-called 'war on drugs', though increasingly controversial, continues to consume colossal resources.

Another substance now subject to considerable control where once it was freely used and enjoyed is tobacco. In societies where it is now illegal to smoke indoors in the workplace, in bars and restaurants, or even in cars with children in them, it is increasingly difficult to imagine a time when tobacco was promoted as a health product. In the late 1940s, the RJ Reynolds tobacco company in the US launched an advertising campaign with the slogan 'More doctors smoke Camels than any other cigarette'. As evidence accumulated on the negative health impact of smoking during the 1950s it became increasingly difficult to use the medical profession in this way. It was the mid-1990s, however, before

California became the first state to institute a smoking ban on all enclosed workplaces including bars and restaurants. By no means all states have such bans—indeed over twenty have no state-wide ban, and the extraordinary patchwork of laws and regulations that restrict smoking in some locations in particular parts of America but not others is perhaps a perfect illustration of how the law is not a straightforward guide to which behaviours we consider problematic and wish potentially to punish.

The final example concerns rape within marriage. In the US, it is now illegal in all fifty states, but that has been the case only since 1993. The process of criminalization of marital rape began in the mid-1970s, but it was almost two decades before it was outlawed across the whole of the country. In England, there was no such offence until 1991. The change in the law in 1991 brought England into line with a range of other countries including France, Canada, Sweden, Denmark, Norway, the Soviet Union, and Australia. Prior to this shift, as one English Judge put it in the 17th century:

> A husband cannot be guilty of rape committed by himself upon his lawful wife, for by their mutual matrimonial consent and contract the wife hath given up herself in this kind unto her husband, which she cannot retract.

Although women's rights have led to the criminalization of marital rape in much of the developed world, there remain numerous countries where no such offence exists. The *Times of India*, for example, reported in late 2016 that the country's Home Affairs minister, Haribhai Chaudhary, had said that marital rape could not be criminalized in India because of the high illiteracy rate, poverty, extreme religious beliefs, and the 'sanctity' of marriage. One international study has suggested that intimate partner violence is, globally, the most common form of violence experienced by women and in consequence scholars have recently argued that criminalizing sexual violence against women in intimate relationships ought to be a central plank in 'the human rights agenda for achieving gender equality'. Marital rape neatly illustrates not only that standards change over time with some matters that were once not punishable now being brought within the ambit of the criminal law, but also the reality that there is often considerable variation jurisdiction to jurisdiction. A few other quick illustrations of the latter point.

Over twenty countries in the world continue to have apostasy laws: laws punishing people for abandoning or renouncing their religious faith. These countries are mainly in Africa, the Middle East, and South/Southeast Asia, and many have laws against apostasy which carry the death penalty, though only Iran in recent years appears to have executed anyone convicted of such a crime. A wider array of countries—as varied as India, Ireland, Kuwait, the Philippines, and Poland—continue to have blasphemy laws, punishing expressions considered to have insulted, defamed, or expressed contempt for sacred things. In much of the world, however, such laws are considered to be incompatible with human rights considerations. Indeed, the United Nations has taken the view that because 'freedom of religion or belief' and 'freedom of speech' are both important human rights, blasphemy laws should therefore be considered a 'problematic restriction'.

Another form of activity that is subject to varying forms of regulation is prostitution. Indeed, here we need to think rather more subtly than simply distinguishing between jurisdictions that permit such activity and those that don't. Countries that criminalize prostitution can be said, broadly speaking, to take three slightly differing positions. First, there are those that attempt so far as practicable to *prohibit* prostitution by criminalizing every aspect of the activity. By contrast there is the *abolitionist* position that views prostitution as a social problem, but one requiring legal intervention only where public safety or social order are in some way threatened. There is a linked subcategory of abolitionism that focuses its concerns not on prostitutes but on others such as pimps and clients. Jurisdictions taking a more tolerant, or less interventionist, approach can be divided into those that *decriminalize* prostitution, regulating it by means other than the criminal law, and those that specifically *legalize* such activity, treating it similarly to all other occupations.

Finally in relation to criminalization there is what we might call 'developmental relativity' or age-graded law. We don't treat all humans in the same way when it comes to criminal justice. Most obviously, we distinguish between adults, juveniles, and younger children. Adults, with certain exceptions, we treat as if they are capable of being held entirely responsible for their actions. Juveniles, by contrast, we generally give a little more leeway, assuming that they require a little more protection and greater care than we allow for adults that have transgressed. Finally, in most jurisdictions there is an age cut-off below which people are not held to be criminally liable for their conduct. This is generally referred to as the 'age of criminal responsibility' and the fact that it varies from country to country—from as low as 7 in some US states (and up to 12 in others) to 10 in England, Wales, and Australia, 15 in Denmark, 16 in Spain, and 18 in Brazil—illustrates much of what we have been saying thus far.

More generally, countries vary markedly in their treatment of particularly young offenders. In 1993, in England, a 2-year old boy, James Bulger, was out shopping with his mother. She briefly lost sight of him while she was in a shop. With her attention diverted, James was abducted. After a lengthy search, and a great many hours later, he was found dead near a railway line a few miles away. He had been brutally assaulted. Most shockingly, the two perpetrators were also young boys, both aged 10 at the time of the incident. As the age of criminal responsibility in England at the time was 10 the two boys were, in principle, eligible to stand trial in a criminal court. Just a year later, in Norway in 1994, a 5-year-old girl, Silje Redergard, was assaulted by two 6-year-old boys—friends she had been playing with—so seriously that she died of her injuries. In Norway, the age of criminal responsibility is 15 so there was no question of a prosecution and criminal trial. In that respect the cases are not at all comparable. But there is more about the cases that is revealing. In Norway, huge effort went into protecting the two boys, ensuring that their identities were never revealed, and that they received help and support. Nationally, the case was viewed as a one-off, a tragic case, and one that necessitated expert intervention. By contrast, the two perpetrators in the Bulger case were quickly identified, were subject to extremely hostile treatment in the media, were seen as symptomatic of a wider and deeper problem in British society, were tried in court, and were sentenced to lengthy prison terms. Though not solely a story about the age of criminal responsibility, the two cases offer a clear contrast in the ways in which different jurisdictions treat crimes involving the young. Perhaps an even greater contrast would have been visible had such a crime taken place in the US. There, the likelihood is that the perpetrators would have served much lengthier prison sentences—they were released at age 18 in England—perhaps never to have been discharged from prison.

The focus of criminal justice

Another observation we might make from these two cases is that via the criminal justice process—police, prosecutors, and courts—we *construct* criminals. That is to say, we take people and through a process of arresting, charging, prosecuting, and, when there is a finding of guilt, imposing a sentence, we label them as 'criminal'. One of the great contributions, perhaps the greatest contribution, of sociological criminology in the mid-20th century, was to focus attention on a process that I have already referred to as *criminalization*. By focusing on the ways in which the label 'crime/criminal' is attached to certain behaviours and, consequently, to certain people, we can illustrate clearly why crime should be seen as socially constructed. If we begin from this perspective we are forced to ask how certain behaviours become defined as deviant or criminal, why particular individuals or groups are more or less likely to be those to whom the label deviant/criminal is applied, and to ask what the consequences of applying such labels might be. Had the age of criminal responsibility in England in 1993 been 12, the two young perpetrators in the Bulger case could not have been prosecuted. Some other form of intervention would have had to have taken place and they would not have been defined as 'criminal'. Would their lives have been different as a consequence? Almost certainly.

Asking questions about what/who becomes labelled as a 'crime'/'criminal' necessarily invites one to contemplate the importance of power. Who makes the rules? Who do the rules affect, or protect? Are the rules applied equally and, if not, why is that and what are the consequences? Perhaps the easiest way to do this is to take any major social division—income and wealth, gender, and ethnicity, for example—and then look at how the law is enforced. Let us take two quick examples. First, the use of a basic police power: what is called 'stop and frisk' in America and 'stop and search' in the UK. Who do the police tend to stop? In 2015, in New York City, a total of 22,939 stops were made by police officers. Of the people that were stopped, 12,223 were black (54 per cent); 6,598 were Latino (29 per cent), and 2,567 were white (11 per cent). This in a city where according to its census well over 40 per cent of its citizens are white and about one-quarter are black. Official data in England and Wales show that the stop and search rate (the number of people stopped and searched per 100,000 population) is approximately fifteen for white people and sixty-five for black people. In other words a more than 400 per cent difference.

The ways in which certain groups tend to be disproportionately criminalized—to find themselves much more likely to be prosecuted and punished—potentially illustrates something important about social attitudes and generalized assumptions that are held about certain groups or categories of people. Let us take the example of indigenous Australians. Broadly speaking, it seems that indigenous adults in Australia are nearly fourteen times as likely as non-indigenous people to be imprisoned. The detention rate for indigenous juveniles is nearly 400 per 100,000, almost thirty times higher than the rate for non-indigenous juveniles. What are the reasons for this? One possibility, of course, is that they are more heavily involved in crime. There is some evidence to support this, though such over-involvement is in all likelihood explained by the greater concentration of 'risk factors' (we will explore such factors in more detail in Chapter 3) among these population groups. At least as importantly, if not much more so, is the deliberate targeting of such people by the police and other authorities. One study in New South Wales (NSW) found that by the age of 23 more than three-quarters of the indigenous population had been cautioned by the police, referred to a youth justice 'conference', or convicted of an offence in court. By contrast, the figure for the non-indigenous population was 17 per cent. It will perhaps therefore not come as a shock to discover that the number of indigenous Australians in NSW prisons more than doubled between 2001 and 2015.

The second example of the differential focus of the criminal justice system concerns the response of authorities to different types of financial fraud. In England, the responsibility for collecting taxes and for investigating compliance is undertaken by Her Majesty's Revenue and Customs (HMRC). Among taxpayers there is a small group, estimated at 0.02 per cent of all taxpayers, who are labelled 'high net worth individuals'. The amount of tax around which there are considered to be 'risks'—essentially of tax avoidance or, possibly, evasion by these individuals runs into the billions of pounds sterling. In the five years to 2016, seventy cases were investigated, two criminally investigated, and one eventually resulted in a successful criminal prosecution. By contrast, around 8,000 to 9,000 people are successfully prosecuted every year for what is referred to as benefit fraud—falsely claiming a welfare benefit to which they are not entitled or failing to report changes in their personal circumstances—with about 5 per cent of such cases ending in a prison sentence. Where the richest offenders are concerned, prosecutions are rare and even then the state is most concerned with recovery of losses, not with other forms of punishment. Now, part of the explanation for this concerns the difficulty in securing successful prosecutions in such cases. Nevertheless, it remains the case that where the poorest offenders are concerned, criminal prosecution is very much more likely, despite the much smaller losses involved.

The most accurate estimate suggests that benefit fraud, in sum, might reach close to £2.4 billion per annum. By contrast, the same source suggests that private sector fraud, at a conservative estimate, costs the UK economy over £140 billion per annum. As I have said, prosecutions are rare, and much corporate harm is dismissed as being the unfortunate side effect of successful enterprise. As a number of criminologists have done, it is possible to take a very different view, seeing the problems caused by corporations as being anything but marginal aberrations or deviations, but rather as core to their functioning. Given the threat they are argued to pose to our well-being, the implication is that we must challenge their very existence.

Crime or harm?

Thus far we have looked a little at the concept of *crime*, asked a series of questions about what it might mean, and, I hope, illustrated that it is not as straightforward an idea as it might seem at first. Indeed, as I suggested earlier there are those that see it as being so problematic that they question the whole enterprise of criminology. Is there an alternative? Well, the most usual suggestion is that we should shift our focus from *crime* to *harm*. One reason for arguing this is the suggestion that crime, the core subject of criminology, has no *ontological reality*. What is meant by this is the fairly straightforward idea that the range of behaviours, actions, events, and so on that we label 'criminal' have nothing essential in common other than the fact that we label them as criminal. That is to say, it implies a false coherence, and gives a sense that the things we criminologists study belong together, when the reality is quite different. What is there, for example, that links drink driving, prostitution, cannabis use, rape, identity theft, and serial murder (other than they feature in the criminal law)?

As a consequence, we may make the same point in relation to one of the other main objects of study in criminology: *criminals*. The term implies that these people share something, that they have something in common. Now, in one sense they do, they must have been found guilty of a criminal offence to be labelled a criminal. But do they share anything beyond that? We often talk publicly and politically, and indeed behave, as if they do. And there have been, and remain, some criminologists who appear to think along these lines. But let's take a step back. Can *criminals* somehow be a class apart, different constitutionally (genetically, biologically, psychologically, socially) from *non-criminals*? There are approximately 250 million adults in the United States. Like to guess how many, roughly (it is difficult to know with accuracy), have a criminal record? One million? Ten million? No, it is thought that sixty-five million adults in the United States have a criminal record. That is, over a quarter of all adult Americans have been convicted of at least one criminal offence, albeit that most of these offences are relatively minor and not the most serious crimes. And, of course, such things are not evenly distributed so the proportion would be significantly higher for some ages/groups.

Still think that it is possible that *criminals* (someone with a criminal record) could be constitutionally different from *non-criminals*? Probably not is my guess. Just in case I've not convinced you yet, let me illustrate for you the utter absurdity of treating 'criminals' as if they were a separate category of people—somehow physically, morally, or dispositionally different from the rest of us. Ask yourself one simple question: have I or has anyone in my immediate family committed at least one of the following acts: smoked cannabis; driven a car with excess alcohol in the bloodstream; stolen something from a shop; downloaded music or other material for free when it should have been paid for?

Now, there are only four offences there out of the tens of thousands of possibilities. But even with this very limited list did you answer 'no'? If you did—congratulations—you are part of a tiny minority of people who will have done so. The reason is straightforward. All these things, any of which could, in principle, lead to criminal charges, are very common. It is not easy estimate what proportion of the population have done any of those listed acts, but we can make some estimates. Here goes:

- *Smoked cannabis*—the World Drug Report suggests that the proportion of people using cannabis at least once annually was 5 per cent in Germany, 12 per cent in Canada, 15 per cent in Italy and New Zealand. Lifetime measures of cannabis use are of course even higher. The Crime Survey for England and Wales suggests over one-third (36 per cent) of adults have used an illicit drug at some point in their lives.

- *Driven a car with excess alcohol in the bloodstream.* In self-report surveys, somewhere between one-quarter and one-half of respondents report having driven within a few hours of having had an alcoholic drink. Now, this doesn't mean they were 'over the limit', but in all likelihood it does mean that they were at risk.

- *Stolen from a shop.* Self-report studies, of which there are quite a few, report quite widely differing results, but the most reliable studies report findings between 25 and 50 per cent.

- *Downloaded music or other material for free when it should have been paid for.* Again, as you might appreciate, this is difficult to estimate. One report from Australia, a country which has a population of approximately twenty-three million, estimated that almost three million Australians visited the top two downloading sites in one month in 2014. That's not to say they all, or even most of them, actually downloaded material illegally. On the other hand, it was only one month in one year, and only two of the thousands of sites.

At the very least, this brief discussion should, I hope, have convinced you that we need to be very careful when discussing terms like *crime* and *criminal*, certainly when addressing them in the most general terms.

But what about the more specific question of whether it is possible to distinguish the most serious offenders—murderers and rapists, for example—from other people? Again, though the answer is effectively *no*, the picture is a complex one. There is a large, and growing, body of work that suggests that there may be a number of risk factors associated with the more serious, and less frequent, forms of criminal conduct. For example, what is often referred to as 'early onset' offending—essentially starting early in life—is strongly linked with an increased likelihood of a lengthy involvement in crime later in life as well as a heightened likelihood of involvement in serious, violent, or dangerous crime. A number of family factors, notably family break-up, violence within the home, and being placed in care outside the family, are all associated with increased risk of later serious and violent offending. Similarly, early alcohol or other substance abuse is another key risk factor.

In addition to these matters, criminologists are now increasingly turning their attention to biological and psychological factors in the explanation of serious offending, especially very serious violent offending. In some respects this marks a return to some of the preoccupations of the early criminologists in the late 19th and early 20th centuries. Interest in such matters became much less common in the second half of the 20th century—indeed deeply unfashionable—but what are now often termed *biosocial* factors are firmly back on the criminological agenda. Again, such work identifies a range of features that appear to be associated with a heightened propensity towards the more serious forms of crime, especially violence, and towards extended involvement in crime. These risk factors include a number of neuropsychological or cognitive deficits such as poor organizational skills and limited attention span, low intelligence and working memory, together with other traits such as impulsivity and displays of aggression early in life. In addition, there are a number of very early life factors, such as birth complications and disruptions to brain development caused by smoking and alcohol consumption during pregnancy, that are associated with violence, and sometimes extreme violence, later in life. Crucially, however, only some of those individuals displaying such characteristics will go on to offend to any serious degree. The risk factors are important influences rather than distinguishing characteristics or determining features. We will return to these and related issues in Chapter 3.

Despite an arguably understandable preoccupation among the public and in the media with the most serious forms of crime, the reality is that the vast majority of matters considered criminal are fairly trivial (that is to say, they cause little harm). This raises the important question of what the criminal justice and penal systems are set up to achieve. Are they there to punish, and if possible deter, those behaviours that we think of as the worst, the most serious, causing the most harm and damage? And, if not, what are they doing?

Within that body of matters called crime, it is rarely the most serious that end up in the criminal justice system. This might seem surprising but can be illustrated in two ways. First and most straightforwardly, there are harms caused by nation states through acts of violence or appropriation. Some of these may be governed by international standards, treaties, and legislation, but a great many will not be. Even if potentially labelled as 'criminal' and punishable in international tribunals, the likelihood of such prosecution is very rare indeed. The Center for Constitutional

Rights, a human rights non-governmental organization (NGO) based in New York has, for example, described the lawbreaking undertaken by the administration of President George W. Bush as 'monumental in scope'. Archbishop Desmond Tutu called for both President Bush and ex-British Prime Minister Tony Blair to face war crime charges in the Hague. Though Archbishop Tutu has been far from alone in making such a call, there are few who imagine that either former leader will find themselves in the dock in the Netherlands. Second and as suggested earlier, many harms perpetrated by, say, companies and corporations, while potentially criminal, are rarely prosecuted. Increasing attention in recent years has been focused on the great many environmental harms perpetrated by corporations around the globe. One report for the United Nations calculated that in 2008 the top 3,000 public companies were responsible for $2.15 trillion worth of environmental damage. The report also suggested that, however good these companies may look on paper, if they were held responsible for the damage they caused they would lose at least half of their profits. Some would simply fold. An increasingly large body of work, often referred to as *green criminology*, now focuses upon such environmental 'crimes'.

Finally, as a consequence of such shortcomings critics then remind us, perhaps not surprisingly, that criminal justice is not terribly effective. Crime rates often remain stubbornly high even when both the quantity and the harshness of punishment is increased, and individual reoffending or recidivism is generally similarly high despite the use of imprisonment and other forms of punishment. Worse than this, the consequence of resorting to the use of the criminal justice system, critics argue, is that less formal, and potentially more effective, means of dealing with conflict are neglected. When a matter—let's say a dispute between neighbours that ends in minor violence—is defined as a criminal matter a number of things are set in train. The tendency is to treat one party as an *offender* and one as a *victim*. Things are often not nearly so clear cut as this with obvious consequences for fairness and justice. Once charges are brought, the victim is largely excluded from the remainder of proceedings. This in itself may cause hurt and distress. Finally, in the example we have used the matter that led to proceedings—the dispute between neighbours—may well not be settled by taking matters to court and, indeed, could potentially be made an awful lot worse. Missing the opportunity to resolve conflicts by other means, some argue, is a very great loss to society. It is precisely such observations, in part, that have led to the growth in interest in alternative justice systems—restorative justice, for example—and in a variety of other forums such as truth and reconciliation commissions, and their like.

So, how should we conclude? First, we need to treat the idea of *crime* with considerable caution. We must be aware of the dangers of lumping together highly disparate acts as if they necessarily have characteristics in common. The same applies to the term *criminal*. As a consequence, we must be wary of imposing too strict a boundary on what passes as the subject matter of criminology. Yes, criminologists are interested in *crime*, but in the very broad senses outlined in this chapter and not to the exclusion of other concerns. Our next question is who commits crime?

Chapter 3
Who commits crime?

How might we answer this question? Well, perhaps the most obvious would be to look at who is arrested by the police, and who is prosecuted and punished. That is to say, to understand *who* commits crime we could look at who is processed by the criminal justice system. And, indeed, there are lots of good reasons why we could start like this. The criminal justice system—police, courts, prisons, probation, and so on—are the institutions that we have created in modern times to respond to *crime*.

The use of criminal records reinforces the point made in the last chapter that a significant proportion of the population will acquire a conviction in their lifetime. One classic early longitudinal research study found that about one-third of males born in 1945 in Philadelphia had experienced police contact by the age of 18. The Pittsburgh Youth Study conducted much more recently found that about one-quarter of the cohort had been arrested for violence by the age of 19, and about 20 per cent had been arrested for serious theft. A sizeable analysis conducted by the British government found that approximately one-third of males (33 per cent) and something under 10 per cent of females had a criminal conviction by their mid-30s.

Again, we ought to pause here for these figures are worthy of a little more scrutiny. If you were to ask members of the public what proportion of men they thought had a criminal conviction—that is had been arrested, prosecuted, and found guilty in a criminal court—my guess is that most would come up with a figure below—and possibly way below—one-third. That the proportion is so high also gives the lie to the idea that 'criminals' are some sort of *other*, different from the mainstream population. Quite the contrary in fact. Now, as we observed in Chapter 2, this is to focus on crime in general. Perhaps we would come up with a different answer if we focused on specific types of crime? We return to this question when we consider serious and persistent offenders later in this chapter.

Although using arrest or conviction data offer some interesting findings, having got this far in the book you might already be spotting a problem—or at least a limitation—in relying on such information. We know that not all crime comes to the attention of the police and therefore finds its way into the criminal justice system (and we'll look at this in greater detail in Chapter 4). Indeed, official data from the UK has shown that an offender is identified in less than 6 per cent of all crimes. Given such limitations, what is the alternative? The answer is survey methods, or what is called the 'self-report' approach, where people are quizzed about their criminal conduct. To what extent are people honest about such matters? you might rightly ask. In fact, scientific assessments over many years tend to conclude that self-report studies, if well-conducted, are broadly reliable and valid.

One of the longest-standing pieces of self-report research is a British study, the Cambridge Study in Delinquent Development, which for over half a century now has been following the lives of over 400 males, using a combination of face-to-face interviews and an analysis of their criminal records. The boys all came from a relatively poor, working-class area of London. Predictably, self-reported prevalence of offending was high, with the Cambridge study finding that three-quarters of males aged 10–18 had committed at least one of eight selected offences. The vast majority of males (94 per cent) reported at least one offence in their lives up until their late 40s. Such findings are broadly replicated in other major self-report studies and show, to put it simply, that offending is quite common and is not restricted to a small minority of the population.

Quite common it may be but, generally speaking, it is also something of a youthful specialism. Indeed, the existence of an 'age-crime curve' is something that criminologists feel they can talk about with a high degree of certainty. The age-crime curve refers to the fact that criminal activity and other antisocial behaviour is increasingly likely during adolescence, tends to peak around the late teens, and declines quite quickly thereafter, with relatively few people continuing to offend into their 30s, 40s, or beyond. This general pattern has been found in research in different countries, at different points in time, for men and women, and across all ethnic groups. Indeed, so strong is this relationship between age and crime that the age-crime curve is often described as a 'universal finding'.

In addition to age, and as we have already seen, there are very significant differences in offending patterns by gender. Men are responsible for the bulk of offending and predominate at all stages of the criminal justice system. Uniform Crime Report (UCR) data from the US—collected from law enforcement agencies—suggest that women make up somewhere between 10 and 20 per cent of all arrestees within most offence categories. The highest proportion, at a little under two-fifths, is for fraud. Vandalism and aggravated assault are the only other categories where women make up over one-fifth of arrestees. For homicide the figure is just over one-tenth.

Again, such differences are replicated in self-report studies. A very early study undertaken in the city of Sheffield in the UK, asked juveniles questions about a range of activities. Some of these were criminal, others deviant but possibly not criminal. On some matters—occasional truancy from school, vandalism, and theft from school—there were only minor differences between the boys and girls. However, in relation to clear criminal offences—burglary, shoplifting, violence—the proportion of boys reporting involvement was significantly higher. A more recent and larger study in New Zealand, looking at a cohort of 1,000 males and females found consistent differences between them throughout early life to age 21, with males predominating at all ages, though greater similarities between the sexes were found in relation to antisocial behaviour during mid-adolescence, and in their drug- and alcohol-related offending. Nevertheless, the consistent picture presented by research is that offending is primarily a youthful activity, and it is one that is disproportionately undertaken by boys or men.

What about race and ethnicity? Self-report studies demonstrate higher levels of involvement in offending among some minority populations, particularly among black people, though such differences tend to disappear when socio-economic status is taken into account. We know that some ethnic minorities tend to be disproportionately likely to be represented at most if not all stages of the criminal justice process, from arrest to imprisonment. Black people are almost six times as likely to be arrested for robbery as white people in the United States for example, five times as likely to be arrested for murder, and more than twice as likely to be arrested for property crimes in general. Generally, two different types of explanation are offered for such huge disparities. Some suggest that this is a result of greater involvement in crime by black people and, especially, in the types of crime that lead to the attention of the police. Such heightened involvement may be a consequence of many things, from the general social and educational disadvantage experienced by such groups through to the development of an oppositional street culture that heightens the likelihood of conflict with those in authority such as the police.

Robert Sampson and his colleagues in their study of Chicago neighbourhoods sought an explanation for the fact that the odds of perpetrating violence were 85 per cent higher for black people compared with white people, while Latino perpetrated violence was 10 per cent lower. They found neighbourhood social context to be a highly significant factor in explaining such disparities. Their conclusion was that social segregation was closely linked to exposure to many of the key risk factors (poverty, family breakdown, poor educational opportunities, etc.) and protective factors (high educational expectations, association with non-delinquent peers, etc.) associated with crime. In short, as a consequence of where they lived poor, black youth had much greater exposure to key risk factors and far less to the main protective factors.

Rather than focus on differences in involvement in crime an alternative explanation rests on the argument that there is a process of selection involved in the way that the criminal justice system is organized and that this focuses official attention on particular groups. More particularly, from this perspective it is argued that the organization and operation of the police leads to the targeting of people of colour and that subsequent police, prosecutorial, and sentencing practices lead to heightened rates of arrest, conviction, and punishment; in short it is a story of differential and discriminatory treatment within the criminal justice process. A third possibility is that some combination of both these positions—differential involvement and system selection—explains the over-representation of minorities with the justice system. Though there is no consensus among criminologists in the attempt to explain such differences, it is the third possibility that appears to command most support.

So, before we move on, a quick summary. From both official criminal justice and from self-report data we know that offending is far from uncommon—in the sense that most of us have committed some offences, albeit not terribly serious ones, at some point in our lives. Furthermore, a significant proportion of the population will have at least one criminal conviction by the time they reach middle age. But we also know that there are other patterns to offending. First and foremost, most offending is done by the young, and from the late teenage years onwards offending tends to decline in most people's lives. Second, it is also predominantly a male activity. Across most crime types, significantly higher proportions of boys/men will be involved than is the case for girls/women. Third, some minority ethnic groups appear to have higher offending rates than others, though it seems likely that some combination of social and economic inequality, and the way in which the criminal justice and penal systems work, hold the key to explaining much of the difference.

What about income/wealth, social status, social class? How are these related to offending? Well, we know that the vast majority of crimes dealt with by the criminal courts are committed by people of relatively impoverished means. Indeed, the predominance of people of lower social status in offending can be seen irrespective of how offending is measured. As the Australian criminologist, John Braithwaite, simply observed: 'lower-class adults commit those types of crime which are handled by the police at a higher rate than middle-class adults'. But the key phrase here is 'those types of crime handled by the police'. What about the crimes of the socially advantaged? As mentioned earlier, a body of hugely important work within criminology in recent years has attempted to shift the focus of academic (and social) attention to 'social harms'—whether these be physical, psychological, emotional, or economic harms. Such an approach, it is argued, allows attention to be paid to otherwise ignored problems such as workplace injury and death, environmental offences, corporate 'offences' and other forms of white-collar crime, and the 'crimes' committed by states.

White-collar offending

The gaze of the state, and that of academic criminologists, tends to focus on the crimes of the powerless, rather than the powerful, despite the very great harms caused by the latter. What do we know about those who commit white-collar crime? Predictably enough their demographic characteristics differ somewhat from the typical profile of someone convicted of burglary, violence, theft, and criminal damage—in other words, those crimes that tend to fill our criminal courts. For the purposes of this discussion we'll call these latter crimes 'street crimes'. White-collar offenders tend to be older and—at least as measured by when they get their first criminal conviction—appear to start their offending later in life, often as late as their late 30s/early 40s. In part, this may reflect the relative complexity of some of the crimes, and the degree of workplace or professional seniority necessary before the crime can be committed. Data on the ethnicity of white-collar offenders is pretty thin and, in the main, suggests that, in the West, white offenders tend to predominate, particularly among the more serious forms of crime.

One variable that is pretty consistent across both 'street crime' and white-collar crime is gender: women form very much the minority of offenders in both cases. Where women are involved in white-collar offending, research suggests that it is mostly at the lower levels, particularly involving crimes such as smaller scale embezzlement. To some degree this may reflect the opportunities available as a consequence of the different occupational profiles of men and women in the business world. As far as the class background of offenders is concerned, almost by definition it will be the case that the bulk of white-collar offenders will be classified as 'middle-class' by virtue of being in relatively well-paid employment. However, as we begin to learn more about the Internet-facilitated forms of fraud that now appear to be occurring with increasing frequency, it may be that our picture of the social backgrounds of fraudsters may change (whether we will still consider 'white-collar crime' to be a useful descriptor is another point).

Let us finish this section by reflecting briefly on the scale of the harm that can be involved in such offending. Estimating the costs of white-collar crime is notoriously difficult—not least because victims will often not know that they have been the subject of a crime. Nevertheless, such figures as are available are staggering. Occupational theft and employee fraud in the US is estimated to cost $800 billion a year—and this is only the costs to victims and not the associated costs of prevention and prosecution. The respective figure for counterfeiting products and piracy is over $200 billion and between $40 and $80 billion for each of insurance fraud, retail fraud, and health insurance fraud.

One estimate put the total cost of 'street crime' victimization—the more usual crimes of violence, burglary, theft, and so on that dominate the criminal courts—in the US at approximately $834 billion, or something similar to the total just cited for occupational theft and employee fraud. In fact, it is suggested that the total victimization costs of white-collar crime may exceed $1.6 trillion, and that even this ignores the losses resulting from the psychological impact of such crimes. In short, it seems highly likely that the costs of white-collar crime far exceed those of street crime, and yet they have much less impact on criminal justice and assume far less significance in terms of our anxieties or fears about crime, political debate around crime, or, indeed, criminological attempts to measure the extent of crime.

The distribution of offending

We have established that many people may very occasionally offend, albeit at a low level. However, research also shows that a small number will offend frequently and over extended periods of time, and will tend to commit more serious offences. What do we know about the distribution of offending and what do we know about these offenders? One of the consistent findings of criminological research is that there tends to be continuity from childhood and adolescence to adulthood in antisocial behaviour. As one scholar put it, 'adult antisocial behaviour virtually requires childhood antisocial behaviour'. Few begin their criminal involvement in adulthood (white-collar criminals being one obvious exception), but, equally, the majority of antisocial children don't go on to become antisocial adults. Of those that do, however, a small number will account for a disproportionate amount of overall crime. The classic Philadelphia research mentioned earlier calculated that 6 per cent of all the males in the study (about 18 per cent of the offenders) were responsible for over half of all juvenile arrests, and accounted for an even higher proportion of serious offences. The Cambridge study that was also mentioned found that 6 per cent of the males accounted for up to half of all convictions up to age 32.

These so-called 'persistent' or 'chronic' offenders are the source of much criminological and political interest—the assumption being that if it were possible to identify them early on and intervene in their lives somehow, either by diverting them from crime or preventing them offending by imprisoning them, then the knock-on effect on crime reduction would be very substantial. What then do we know of them? We know that these so-called 'chronic offenders' tend to have an early onset of offending, engage in high frequency offending, and have long 'criminal careers'. The risk factors for early onset of offending range from individual matters (low intelligence, low school/educational achievement, hyperactivity, impulsiveness and risk-taking, and childhood antisocial behaviour such as bullying), family circumstances (poor parental supervision, harsh discipline and child physical abuse, child neglect, parental conflict, family break-up, and delinquent siblings), peers (having peers that are themselves in trouble or are rejected by peers/unpopular), to community factors such as living in a high crime neighbourhood.

One influential body of research, associated primarily with the American psychologist Terrie Moffitt, distinguishes between the vast bulk of youthful offenders—those who will offend more or less frequently during their teenage years but whose offending will then decline and quite likely stop as they mature—and a small minority who will continue to offend through their adult years. These she refers to as 'adolescent-limited' and 'life-course persistent' offenders, respectively. The nature of offending by 'life-course persistent' offenders changes over time—perhaps beginning with truancy and shoplifting, later developing via selling drugs, stealing cars, robbery, and violence. The underlying disposition of such individuals is said to remain relatively unchanged, the offending shifting as new opportunities arise as the individuals age. The prospects for such people are poor: with drug and alcohol addiction, poor employment chances, homelessness, high levels of victimization, and, of course, considerable contact with the criminal justice system all being likely.

Beyond their differing offending patterns, what differentiates 'life-course persistent' from 'adolescent-limited' offenders? It is argued that the persistent offenders tend to suffer from a number of neuropsychological deficits. The suggestion is that brain abnormalities as a result of inherited characteristics, of poor pre-natal nutrition, drug abuse, or exposure to other toxic substances, or as a result of abuse are strongly linked to the development of later antisocial tendencies. Moreover, any such raised risk of antisocial and offending behaviour later in life is increased among this group because they are significantly more likely to be born into environments, and live in circumstances, which tend to exacerbate rather mitigate problem behaviours. In short, a chain of events is set in train in the early years which are very difficult to disrupt or shrug off later in life. A number of criminologists have challenged this twofold typology arguing, on the one hand, that the rate of offending of most individuals declines over the life-course, even in so-called 'life-course persistent' offenders and, on the other, that far more than two general patterns or trajectories of offending can be identified. Furthermore and importantly, there continues to be considerable debate over the extent to which it is actually possible to *predict* future patterns of offending among high-risk adolescent delinquents.

Nevertheless, Moffitt's work continues to be hugely influential and is part of the growing interest within criminology in the biosocial factors that influence criminal behaviour. The term *biosocial* is used to indicate that where some form of biological basis for criminal activity can be found, its influence generally works in interaction with the social environment. Using a variety of methods, from studies of identical twins, through brain-imaging to molecular genetics, research into the biological basis of violence in particular is expanding rapidly. Early work, involving studies of identical twins, particularly cases where the twins had been separated, were used to assess the degree of *heritability* involved in antisocial behaviour and aggression, some studies finding that up to half of the variability in levels of antisocial behaviour might be explained by individuals' genetic make-up.

Analytical work using modern imaging technology has identified the prefrontal cortex of the brain as a particularly important focus for research on serious violent crime. Studies have found poor frontal functioning in the brains of murderers, for example, when compared to the brains of others. Why might this matter? The scientists concerned argue that reduced prefrontal functioning is linked with a number of behavioural traits including lowered control of emotions, greater risk-taking, loss of self-control, poor judgement, and a reduced ability to successfully problem-solve, any and all of which might incline someone towards violence. The crucial word here, however, is *incline*. It is not claimed that brain functioning is the determinant of aggressive or violent conduct, merely one component, albeit perhaps an important and still little understood one. No-one seriously disputes that environmental or social factors also play a huge part. For some this remains highly controversial territory, but there can be little doubt that it is one that will see growing interest, and huge developments, in coming years.

Understanding the relationship between biological and social influences is of course crucial. In broad terms, it can be thought of in two ways. The one already mentioned, and the dominant view among most writing currently, is the idea that biological and social factors interact in some way. This is the straightforward idea that biological risk factors—say a particular genetic make-up or poor frontal functioning—combine with familial or social risk factors—such as abusive parenting or relationships with criminal peers—to substantially increase the likelihood that someone will engage in antisocial behaviour. The second is what the neurocriminologist, Adrian Raine, has called the 'social-push' perspective. He uses this term to help explain those cases, found in a number of studies, where children lack those social risk factors that 'push' or predispose them to antisocial behaviour—he uses the example of murderers that grow up in benign home backgrounds. In these circumstances, he argues, it is likely that biological factors are more likely to explain the behaviour concerned. 'You cannot pin the blame on poverty, bad neighbourhoods, or child abuse all the time', says Raine, nor 'is social deprivation so obvious in many more murderers who, while not exactly having heavenly homes as kids, did have homes not much different from yours and mine'. By contrast, he says, where young people are clearly exposed to a number of key social risk factors, it is these factors rather than biological factors that may well be the primary explanation for the behaviour concerned. His argument is not that biology is irrelevant in such cases, merely that its effect is watered down or masked by other influences.

Desistance from crime

The increasing attention paid by criminologists to patterns of offending over the life-course has also led some practitioners to turn their attention to the important question of how we might understand and explain the process of ceasing to offend, or what is increasingly referred to as *desistance*. Early work in this field took the view that the diminution in levels of offending over time was to be explained by the ageing or maturation process—that it was, for a number of possible reasons, a question of 'growing out of crime'—even of 'burnout'. Indeed, desistance occurs primarily in late adolescence/early adulthood. However, some care needs to be taken, for the fact that desistance will occur earlier than this for some offenders and later, possibly much later, for others, means that the relationship between age, maturation processes, and offending patterns is complex. So, what do we know?

As already suggested, desistance from crime is a component part of most offending 'careers'—that is to say, most offenders *do* eventually stop. The incidence of offending declines for most—though not necessarily all—types of offending over time. As we have seen, much research has shown that childhood offending is the best predictor of the pattern of later adult offending, and that the earlier people begin offending the longer their likely criminal career. This has led to a substantial body of work which proposes a broadly 'developmental' argument: suggesting that there are a range of factors that come into play at different stages of life which influence processes towards desistance from crime.

The pathways towards desistance, however, are far from straightforward. One highly influential account links desistance to variations in patterns of informal social control and social bonds that are independent of age. The social bonds refer to the attachments individuals have to socially approved goals and the extent to which they are committed to achieving such goals legitimately. Offending, it is suggested, is more likely when such bonds are weak, and they diminish in likelihood as such bonds increase in strength. Key 'turning points', which can be negative as well as positive, can occur at any stage of life. Positive examples would include events such as getting a job, getting married or entering a relationship, or having children, which help foster social bonds. These, in turn, create systems of obligation and restraint, and make the costs or implications of involvement in crime that much greater. From this perspective, adults develop greater inhibitions in relation to the commission of crime as they accumulate social capital as a result of increasing work and family ties—regardless of their offending history. Now, in one sense this might sound very much like a straightforward argument about development or 'maturation'. It differs though in at least one crucial respect. Rather than implying some form of linear and predictable pattern of maturation, this perspective is based on the assumption that the life-course is unpredictable and that the social contexts that facilitate or impede criminality are ever-present variables that may impinge on individuals' lives at different points and in different ways.

Who commits crime?

Most of us break the law at some point in our lives: men much more than women; a great many young people, especially during their teenage years, though the vast majority of them then give up. There are a few prolific offenders whose offending continues well into their adult years, indeed possibly for much of their lives. Given the disproportionate impact on crime levels that this small group has, it is often thought that one of the keys to reducing crime levels lies in identifying such individuals and intervening in their lives in ways that will somehow prevent or mitigate their offending. This is, however, easier said than done, for identifying in advance those likely to go on to become prolific offenders is a far from straightforward task. The growth of interest in genetics and other biological factors raises the prospect of using a variety of scanning techniques to try to identify potential future serious criminals. Here, the ethical problems are at least as great as the practical ones.

In answer to our question, 'who commits crime?', once again we have to be careful with our terminology. What do we mean when we talk of crime here? In truth, most of the time when we pose such questions we are actually thinking of those types of crimes that most frequently come before our criminal courts—the broad sweep of crimes of theft, damage, and violence, those we have referred to (rather inaccurately, in truth) as 'street crime'.

In putting our focus here we, like our justice systems, are consequently tending to ignore crimes by corporations and the wealthy. The answer to our question is slightly different in relation to these crimes—what some refer to as the 'crimes of the suites' as opposed to crimes of the streets. In terms of offenders, we are still talking about men predominantly, but in such cases they would tend to be older, richer (of course), and much less likely to be subject to arrest, prosecution, and punishment. That they are relatively unlikely to be subject to criminal sanctioning, despite the often substantial overall harm they would appear to be responsible for, arguably not only tells us much about our criminal justice systems, but also about ourselves.

Chapter 4
How do we measure crime?

In Chapter 2, we considered the question 'what is crime?' Bearing in mind all the provisos that were raised in that discussion—not least that the broad term *crime* hides an enormous range of behaviours and is, at best, often very difficult to pin down—we turn our attention now to the question of measurement. What members of the public and politicians generally want to know is, 'how much crime is there?' Is crime—either in general or in relation to particular crimes—going up or down? In what follows, I want to say a little about the main measures that are generally used for counting crime, to look at the pros and cons of different approaches, and to outline a series of qualifications or caveats—basically 'health warnings'—reminding us once again that nothing is quite as it seems.

In much of the world, the closest that anyone gets to a measure of crime is figures that are produced by law enforcement agencies—usually the police. Given that police forces are quite variable in their degree of professionalism and organization, any such statistics will also vary in the ways in which they are created and, consequently, in the degree of reliability that might be placed upon them. Even in jurisdictions with highly professional police forces, and clear rules for the collection and maintenance of such statistics, they are still subject to considerable shortcomings. As a consequence, in some countries in relatively recent times, alternative sources of evidence have been sought. The most usual alternative is to use modern survey methods to ask a large and representative sample of people whether they have been victims of crime, and then to use statistical techniques to estimate likely crime rates for the population as a whole. Although criminologists tend to see this latter approach as the more reliable means of estimating trends over time, they too are not without their problems. We'll investigate those too.

Measurement begins

First, however, a tiny bit of history. When and where were the first national criminal statistics collected and published? The answer lies somewhere in the early to mid-19th century, and the location was France. French systems of punishment were changing, a professional gendarmerie was emerging, and there remained considerable worry about crime and about the so-called 'dangerous classes' in post-revolutionary times. Passports and identity cards were introduced, and the French state gradually developed other means of documenting the population, including these 'dangerous classes', initially by studies of prison conditions. The first statistical inquiries into crime were initiated in 1825 and published in 1827. These initial inquiries were based on information derived from prosecutors, and covered details of all prosecutions, and verdicts from various tribunals, including police courts. Gradually, information about offenders and victims, where available, was also included.

At this point, the figure of Adolphe Quetelet, a Belgian astronomer, enters the picture. Much influenced by the growing statistical movement during his time in France, Quetelet began working on various demographic topics and in due course became intrigued by crime. Within a short period he was studying the incidence of different categories of crime, and speculating that the relationship between those offences known about and those not known (something we'll return to later) would likely vary according to the seriousness of the offences in question and how assiduous the justice system was in seeking to identify the guilty. He also used the available statistics as the basis for speculations on the causes of crime—poverty, for example—and for identifying patterns in offending by age and sex. Insisting that criminal propensities were distributed throughout the population, and not confined to the dangerous classes as was popularly believed, he was a radical figure indeed.

In the US, New York began to collect judicial statistics as early as 1829 and many other states followed suit in the coming decades. These statistics were basically derived from reports sent by state attorneys or clerks of criminal courts to a senior state official, and were generally of little value. Federal criminal statistics began as part of the 1850 census, and were intended to include information both about prisoners and about the numbers of citizens with criminal convictions. Again, however, little of practical use was collected at this point.

It was 1929 before the largely American International Association of Chiefs of Police (IACP) published a volume entitled 'Uniform Crime Reporting', which examined 'all phases of police records and statistics in so far as these are related to national and state reporting'. As part of its work it developed a classification of offences—seven in all—of 'crimes known to the police': murder; forcible rape; robbery; aggravated assault; burglary; larceny-theft; and motor vehicle theft. Supported by Congress, regular reporting started in 1930, albeit as a voluntary activity, and the returns initially from approximately 400 police agencies across forty-three states were sent to the Federal Bureau of Investigation (FBI) which acted as a clearing house. In 1979, Congress mandated the addition of an eighth offence to the UCR list: arson. Importantly, drug offences were not included in the index crimes, a very significant exclusion when thinking about claims about rises and falls in crime. Further changes were made in the 1980s, when a number of organizations including the Department of Justice, the IACP, FBI, and the relatively newly formed Bureau of Justice

Statistics (BJS) met and proposed a number of amendments including the splitting of data into two categories: Part I index crimes covering the eight major offence categories; and Part II index crimes covering a further twenty-one generally less frequently reported offences. By the early 21st century, FBI UCR data, though still not nationally a mandatory requirement, were being drawn from over 18,000 agencies representing over 90 per cent of the population.

In England the collection of national crime statistics began in the aftermath of the 1856 County and Borough Police Act, the legislation which finally established professional police forces across the country. Earlier in the century, growing concerns about crime had led to calls for the collection of information, and from 1810 the clerks to the courts were instructed to make annual returns in which details of approximately fifty offences were recorded. After further developments in the 1830s, much influenced by the statistical movement associated with Quetelet's work in France, the 1856 Act expanded the statistical returns to include indictable (serious) offences known to the police as well as court and prison returns. Offences were divided into six categories: offences against the person; property offences involving violence; property offences not involving violence; malicious offences against property (arson, machine breaking, etc.); offences against the currency; and miscellaneous offences (including riot, sedition, and treason). By the end of the century the annual returns were based on calendar years, included a commentary by the Criminal Registrar and included figures with offences per 100,000 population to allow for comparison over time. They were recognizably the basis for the general form of 'official' criminal statistics still collected today.

New approaches

In France, the US, the UK, and elsewhere, statistical returns from law enforcement agencies—highly variable and undoubtedly unreliable at first, but gradually subject to increasingly tight control and administration—remained the sole, regular statistical measure of crime well into the third quarter of the 20th century. By this point, however, doubts were increasingly being raised as to their utility. Modern survey techniques had been used for some time to study particular aspects of crime. By 1940 in Finland, a question had been introduced in an opinion poll asking about property crime. The major development was in the United States where the Commission of Law Enforcement and the Administration of Justice established by President Johnson had recommended the creation of a new source of crime statistics, having found a series of limitations besetting the existing UCR system. It recommended the creation of a victimization survey—asking people about their experiences of crime rather than relying on those matters which came to the attention of, and were recorded by, law enforcement agencies.

Piloted in the late 1960s, early results indicated far higher levels of crime than had been measured by the standard means. The National Crime Survey was launched in 1972, and after some redesign in 1991 became known the National Crime Victimization Survey (NCVS). The NCVS is conducted annually, being administered to people aged 12 or older across approximately 90,000 households. Households remain in the survey for three years and all eligible persons are interviewed every six months, either in person or by phone, in up to a total of seven interviews. In this survey people are asked about the number and characteristics of any victimization they may have experienced in the previous six months. The NCVS collects information on personal crimes (rape/sexual assault, robbery, aggravated and other assaults, and personal larceny) and household property crimes (burglary, motor vehicle theft, and other theft) irrespective of whether such matters have been reported to the police.

Australia conducted a victimization survey in 1975, and then subsequently in 1983, 1993, 1998, 2002, and 2005. A review conducted in 2006/7 suggested a need for both more timely or regular information and greater flexibility in the survey, and a redesigned survey began in 2009. It is conducted via personal interview and, as with other such surveys, asks about people's experience of victimization over a range of personal and property crimes. In the UK although a small victimization survey was conducted in three areas of London in the early 1970s, the first national survey, covering England and Wales, was conducted in 1982. Then called the British Crime Survey, it became known as the Crime Survey for England and Wales (CSEW) from 2012, Scotland and Northern Ireland having their own surveys. Conducted every two to three years since its inception, the CSEW became an annual rolling survey in the early 2000s. Finally, since 1989, an International Crime Victim Survey has been conducted every few years, allowing criminologists some insight into differing levels of crime across a range of developed countries.

How reliable are our measures?

Although there are other sources of data, information from law enforcement bodies and victimization surveys represent our two main ways of measuring crime levels and trends. The next issue for us, therefore, is to consider in a little more detail why it was felt necessary to create victimization surveys—what were the perceived problems with police/law enforcement statistics?—and what are the general pros and cons of both methods of measurement? Let's start with the most long-standing: FBI-collated uniform crime reports (UCRs) in the US and police-recorded crime statistics in the UK, and their equivalents elsewhere. There are at least five major 'health warnings' that need to be taken into account when using such statistics.

First, they don't include all crimes. Both UCRs in the US and police-recorded crime statistics in England, for example, exclude a range of more minor offences, including a number of traffic offences. Second, there is the question of consistency. At least in England and Wales, there are only forty-three police areas and all are subject to considerable central oversight. Consequently, it is at least possible in principle that the rules governing how crimes are recorded might be reasonably similar across forces. In the United States, not only do states have different criminal laws, but there are literally thousands of law enforcement agencies, each with the potential for slightly different procedures for recording crimes. The UCR system attempts to impose some systematic order on this array of agencies and procedures, but there is a limit to what can be achieved.

Third, only those matters that come to the attention of the police or law enforcement agencies can make it into the recorded crime statistics. If the matter is never reported, then it will never find its way into the statistical table at the end. Why might people not report crimes? There are a host of reasons. There are those crimes that don't have immediate victims: drunk driving, drugs possession, public order offences, and fare evasion, for example. In these cases it is unlikely that someone will report the offence to the police, and such offences generally only come to light as a result of law enforcement activity. Some matters might simply be considered too trivial—theft of a small amount of money. It may simply be that the victim doesn't believe the police can do anything about the crime, so why bother reporting it? People are sometimes quite doubtful about reporting even serious crimes—like burglary/housebreaking—because of a concern about whether there is any likelihood of a perpetrator being detected. Alternatively, the victim may simply feel the police won't be willing to follow it up—perhaps because they feel they won't be believed or it won't be deemed important enough. They may be scared of reprisals if they do report it, or they may be embarrassed. Now as far as the statistics are concerned this means that a very large number of crimes never make it to the attention of law enforcement agencies. Worse still, public willingness to report crimes isn't stable—it varies over time—and therefore, even allowing for non-reporting, reaching a judgement about trends over time is extraordinarily difficult.

What proportion of all crimes that occur do you think are *never* reported to the police? The answer is over half. Yes, fewer than one in two crimes are reported to law enforcement. For that reason alone we would need to be extremely careful about using such statistics as the basis for our estimates of crime. But, 'wait a minute,' I hear you ask, 'if they are not reported to the police how do we know that they exist?' The answer is: victimization surveys, and we return to this shortly. Back to the other limitations of these crime data.

The fourth 'health warning' concerns the recording of crimes by the police. Just because a matter is reported to the police, one cannot assume that it will necessarily be recorded. The reasons for non-recording are also varied, encompassing both police professional decision-making and less acceptable massaging or 'juking' of the statistics. In terms of professional discretion, officers will often have to assess an account given to them by a victim, and they may conclude that there are either reasons not to believe the account they are given or simply that there is insufficient evidence to suggest an offence has taken place. They might simply feel that the matter has already been satisfactorily dealt with. Beyond these reasons there are a range of murkier police practices that are known to affect recording rates, or at least to have done so in the past. In England, police officers—indeed police forces—have regularly been found systematically to fail to record crimes in order to save themselves work or make themselves look better. As the famous American criminologist, Donald Cressey, once put it, 'police have an obligation to protect the reputation of their cities, and when this cannot be done efficiently under existing legal and administrative machinery, it is sometimes accomplished statistically'. In a similar vein, Jianhua Xu's work on the production of crime statistics in Guangzhou, China, suggests that the great 21st-century crime decline in the area never really occurred, but was the result of the data having been manipulated, in part to help reinforce the legitimacy of the Chinese Communist Party.

Failure properly to record crime has been identified as a major failing with such statistics in a number of jurisdictions. In 2009, an inquiry by the Ombudsman in the Australian state of Victoria concluded that poor administrative systems and practices were responsible for considerable under-recording of crime. In the UK a parliamentary select committee went as far as to publish a report entitled 'Caught Red-handed: Why We Can't Count on Police Recorded Crime Statistics'. In short, it found credible evidence that crime was not being properly recorded by the police; and as a consequence the public was told not to trust these statistics.

The fifth and final major health warning simply concerns police practices in the round. That is to say, it is possible that statistics collected by law enforcement agencies tell us more about the size, nature, and practices of law enforcement agencies than they do about the nature and extent of crime. For example, if we significantly increase the size of our police force, will that reduce crime—via detection and deterrence—or will it increase crime—through the simple principle of having more officers available to detect and record offences? The evidence on these questions is mixed. Currently there seems little indication that more police means more recorded crime. And, though there is some evidence that points to the possibility that more police might mean less crime, it is a far from robust conclusion. The point here is simply that, at the very least, one has to accept that statistics of this sort are inevitably affected by the nature of policing practices, not least in relation to those offences that tend to rely upon police work—from drugs offences to traffic violations—than on victims' reports.

Now, all this brings us back to question raised earlier. How do we know what proportion of crimes are reported to the police? The answer is that we are able to use our other main measure—crime surveys—as the basis for such an estimate. By asking a large and broadly representative sample of the population which, if any, crimes they have experienced in the past six to twelve months, and asking a range of follow-up questions including whether the offence was reported to the police, a calculation of overall levels of crime can be made.

Crime surveys

Crime victimization surveys have quite a number of advantages over police-recorded crime statistics/UCRs and the like. Most obviously, they avoid most of the disadvantages of law enforcement derived numbers. Crime surveys are not dependent on public reporting to the police. They are not affected by whether law enforcement officials record crimes accurately. They include a wide range of crimes—relying on victims' assessments of the offence rather than police officers'—though as we'll see such surveys by no means include all crimes. And crime survey estimates are not directly affected either by police practices and policies, or by the number of police officers available to detect or record crimes. Finally, by virtue of being based on a robust and stable methodology—they are conducted in the same way year after year—they give statisticians a high degree of confidence that changes over time are being measured accurately. It is for these reasons that criminologists tend to rely more on crime survey data than other sources when seeking to estimate levels of, and trends in, crime.

All this said, as with any dataset, once again there are 'health warnings' that must be issued and understood in relation to crime surveys. First, as alluded to earlier, crime surveys also don't count all crimes. Murder or homicide, of course, can't by definition be measured by a victimization survey! Then there are those crimes we referred to earlier that might broadly be thought to be 'victimless', such as the possession of drugs or perhaps the sale of drugs. In these cases there is no-one who is likely to say to a researcher that they were the 'victim' of a crime, and in these cases we tend to rely on self-report studies for our estimates.

There are also those crimes which remain partially hidden from view. Domestic assaults, for example, have for a variety of reasons long been surrounded by shame and secrecy. This may be changing now, though slowly, but it almost certainly remains the case that there is considerable under-reporting of such forms of victimization to crime surveys.

The rise of the Internet in the last couple of decades has led to the creation, and identification, of another problem with crime surveys. In short, it seems crime surveys have simply failed to keep pace with what may be some very significant changes in the nature of crime. Huge amounts of theft and fraud, for example, now take place via the Internet rather than 'face-to-face' or within physical premises. In the main, crime surveys have not asked *specifically* about such types of crime and, anyway, it is by no means always the case that people know that they have been victims of such crime. Slowly, crime surveys are beginning to catch up, but it appears that they may have been seriously undercounting crime for some time. We return to this issue in Chapter 5.

The second set of major issues for crime surveys concern their sampling procedures. In brief, even though huge care is taken to try to ensure that those interviewed are numerous enough to allow generalization, and representative enough to reflect the population at large, there remain quite a number of limitations. First and foremost, they tend to exclude those living in non-standard households: including those rough sleeping, living in caravans, hostels, or homes for the elderly, members of the armed forces in military barracks, students living in university accommodation, and those in prison. In the United States the exclusion of those in prison is a fairly sizeable chunk of the population—just under 1 per cent—and, of course, it is a fraction that is likely to have a very particular experience of crime. Third, such surveys are surveys of individuals. They do not include businesses. A range of crimes, from mundane but common offences like shoplifting to less frequent but potentially enormously damaging offences such as large-scale fraud, will simply not be captured by standard victimization surveys. Some countries—Australia, England, and Wales among them—conduct occasional commercial or business victimization surveys, but these are both irregular and relatively small-scale.

The final major issue for crime surveys concerns the dual problem of victim recall and crime frequency. How do surveys cope with the fact that some people will experience no crime, or very little, but a small minority will be victimized a great number of times and may struggle to remember with any precision when things occurred and with what frequency? Abused women, for example, may be subject to a more or less continuous experience of violence and intimidation, such that distinguishing individual incidents becomes all but impossible. Different surveys use different techniques to cope with what is referred to as *multiple, repeat,* or *series victimizations* but the outcome of all of them is that they undercount crime, and in some cases possibly seriously undercount crime. Indeed, a recalibration of the NCVS to attempt to take account of this undercounting led to estimated increases in overall violent crime of between one-quarter and one-third, and increased estimates of rape and sexual assault by over half. Similar findings have recently emerged in England.

So, what should we conclude? Well, it is clear that in recent times we have put in quite a lot of thought and have spent quite a lot of money measuring crime. Law enforcement generated statistics are now governed much more carefully than has ever previously been the case. As a consequence they are undoubtedly also much more accurate than previously. Equally, the more carefully we manage and scrutinize such statistics the more we reveal their limitations. Despite the work that has gone into improving the reliability of such statistics, there is a clear need for alternative sources of information, and it is here that crime—or victimization—surveys come in. More reliable in a number of respects, these data sources are also by no means unproblematic.

In short, our picture of crime levels and trends is always partial. We are much better informed than we used to be and, to paraphrase Donald Rumsfeld, we know more both about what we know *and* what we don't know. Having several sources of data is almost certainly better than having only one, and adopting a constantly sceptical eye towards any claims made is undoubtedly a sensible stance to take. But being sceptical is not the same as being dismissive. While statistics are never fully reliable, and they can certainly be manipulated at the margins, there is much in our crime data of great value, not least in helping us understand general trends in crime over time. It is to these trends we turn our attention to next.

Chapter 5
Understanding recent trends in crime

What is happening to crime? This is one of the obvious questions that concerns the public. Are things getting better or worse, and in what ways? The first step is to look to see what our different types of measurement tell us about crime trends. If they offer similar pictures then we'll have a degree of confidence that the trends identified bear some relationship to reality. Should they differ in important respects then at the very least this should make us scrutinize the trends even more carefully.

I will focus on four jurisdictions: America, Canada, England and Wales, and Australia. We'll begin with the trends according to law enforcement statistics. The trend in the United States is fairly clear. Crime, with a few exceptions, increased most years from 1960 until it reached a peak around 1991–2 (see Figure 1). Overall in that period, recorded crime more than trebled. Since then, however, crime has mostly been on the decrease and although it has by no means returned to its 1960s levels, it is now something like the level it was in the mid-1970s.

In Canada crime rose, most years, from the early 1960s until again reaching a peak somewhere in the late 1980s/early 1990s. Since then the fall in crime has been both fairly consistent and quite steep, bringing crime back down to its early 1970s levels (see Figure 2).

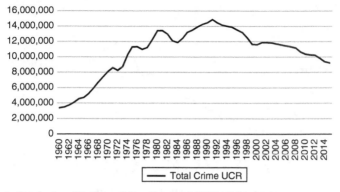

1. Total crime (Uniform Crime Reports), USA, 1960–2015.

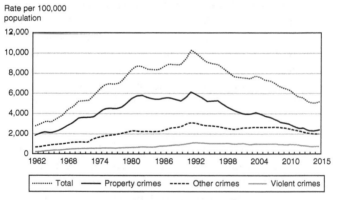

2. Police-reported crime rates, Canada, 1962–2015.

The picture looks a little different in England and Wales—though only at the margins. Again, crime rose consistently and steeply through the 1960s, 1970s, 1980s, and into the 1990s. It appears then, rather like both the US and Canada, to peak somewhere in the early 1990s. However, as the graph makes clear there is a change in data collection techniques—hence the jump in 1997/8—which appears to have crime on an upward trend again until the

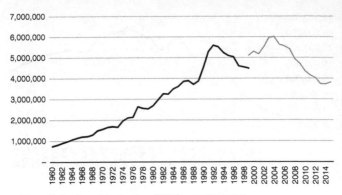

3. Recorded crime, England and Wales, 1960–2015.

early 2000s. Nevertheless, crime then drops steeply, returning to the levels of at least the mid- to late 1980s (see Figure 3). In fact, two artificial changes were made to the ways in which law enforcement derived statistics were collected in England and Wales, both of which inflated the count of crime, and it appears that once those are removed that England and Wales also has a recorded crime rate that has in all likelihood been declining since the early 1990s.

Trends in Australia are somewhat more difficult to piece together as consistent, nationwide figures are difficult to come by. The data that are available suggest that recorded violent and property crime rose through the 1970s and 1980s. Burglary and motor vehicle theft were fairly stable, and even dropped in some states in the 1990s, then fell quickly from the early 2000s. Homicide and robbery also appear to have been falling since the turn of the century, leaving the recorded crime rate some 30–40 per cent lower in 2009 than it had been in the mid-1990s.

So far so good. A quick look at recorded crime trends in four Western democracies shows that they all, to a greater or lesser degree, display similar patterns: rising crime in the post-war years, hitting a peak somewhere between the late 1980s and late 1990s, then falling and falling steeply for the fifteen to twenty-five years since. Though, with the exception of Canada, I've not shown separate figures, it is the case that both the rise and the fall in crime in these countries have tended to affect both violent and property crime. Before we move on to ask *why* crime might have changed in these ways, we ought to double-check the trends by seeing whether our other main source of data—the victimization survey—shows something similar. In the US, the NCVS shows substantial falls in both overall violent crime (rape and sexual assault follows a rather different pattern) and property crimes from the early 1990s. Survey data in Australia have been collected in a much less regular manner, but they are nevertheless consistent with police figures so far as the fall in burglary is concerned. Results on violent crime are less easy to assess. In England and Wales, the CSEW shows overall crime rising from the first survey in 1981 through to the mid-1990s, whereupon it once again begins to fall, and to fall sharply with crime being substantially lower in 2016 than it was when the survey started (see Figure 4).

Given that the two major data sources appear, in very broad brush terms, to be in accord, and that the general trends in the

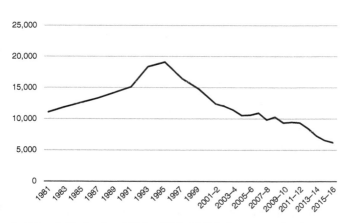

4. **Crime in England and Wales, 1981–2016 (crime survey data).**

four Western democracies studied all appear to be broadly in line, we are left with at least two big questions: first, why did crime increase in the early decades after the Second World War; and, why has it been declining in the past fifteen to twenty-five years?

First, an embarrassing admission—embarrassing for criminologists that is! That crime rose, and rose steadily in the post-war years came as something as a surprise to many. The expectation was that, as societies became more prosperous, as the disruptions of war settled down, and as full or close to full employment was achieved, crime would decline. But as we now know, not only did crime increase, it skyrocketed—certainly as measured by law enforcement derived statistics. Much criminological attention in the late 20th century was then devoted to attempts to explain the crime explosion of the post-war years. We will turn to these explanations shortly. However, at this point the story doesn't get much better. Rather like economists and the financial crash of recent times, criminologists also failed to anticipate the crime decline. Most seemed convinced that there was little and perhaps no prospect at all that the upward trajectory of crime would be reversed. But reversed is precisely what would seem to have happened. The race is now on to explain why crime is in decline—assuming one agrees that it is (not everyone does)—and we will consider this in Chapter 6. First, though, why does there appear to have been such a huge increase in crime from the 1950s and 1960s onward?

The post-war crime explosion

In 1969 in the United States, the President's National Commission on the Causes and Prevention of Violence posed the following question:

Why, we must ask, have urban violent crime rates increased substantially during the past decade when the conditions that are supposed to cause violent crime have not worsened—have, indeed, generally improved? The Bureau of the Census, in its latest report on trends in social and economic conditions in metropolitan areas, states that most 'indicators of well-being point toward progress in the cities since 1960.'

In posing the question this way, the Commission was both making a huge sociological assumption and was also reflecting the view of crime that was held by most experts in America and beyond at the time. The assumption was that, somehow, crime rates were linked to poverty and life chances, and that as post-war prosperity increased so crime would necessarily decline. By the late 1960s, it was clear that a significant crime rise appeared to be underway. Little was the Commission to know that late 1960s' crime rates would pale in comparison with what was on the horizon.

Now, we should pause again and remind ourselves that the only statistics available at this time were police/law enforcement derived figures with all their shortcomings. There are some good reasons to be sceptical about how accurately they were reflecting crime trends in this period. First, it seems more than likely that up to this point there had been relatively little emphasis on recording accuracy—little pressure on police departments to concern themselves with how precisely they were recording what came to their attention. As resourcing of police forces increased so did pressure to act professionally in all regards, including in relation to the collection of information and statistics. It is highly likely therefore that at least some of the recorded increase in crime in the early post-war decades is a consequence of changing police recording practices. Second, alongside rising consumerism, the prosperity of the post-war period brought with it the spread of household and personal insurance (Figure 5), something that is likely to have contributed to the scale of the upward trend in the reporting of crime.

Although there is evidence that insurance companies worked hard, particularly in England, to promote burglary insurance in

5. An advert for Prudential Insurance, 1924.

the early 1900s it really only became widespread in the second
half of the 20th century. Few households were covered prior to
that and, indeed, one very rough estimate made in the 1920s
suggested that only about 5 per cent of all burglary risks in the
United States were covered by insurance. Most successful
insurance claims necessitate contact with the police to report
the loss and, consequently, the spread of insurance all but

guarantees an increase in *the reporting* of crime. There is no easy way of estimating its contribution, but again it seems plausible that an element, and perhaps a sizeable element of the post-war rise in property crime was a consequence of the greater availability of household insurance cover. All this said, it remains highly likely that there were still substantial crime rises in the three decades from the mid- to late 1950s to the 1980s. The next question is why?

In a classic article published in 1979 Lawrence Cohen and Marcus Felson offered what they called a 'routine activities' explanation of elements of the crime rise that had been taking place. Now, they were focusing only on what they referred to as 'direct predatory violations' where 'someone definitely and intentionally takes or damages the person or property of another', but their ideas have broad application. The routine activities approach identifies three components in such criminal events: a motivated offender (someone who wants to commit the crime); a suitable target (someone/something to be attacked/stolen); and, an absence of a 'capable guardian' (inadequate control systems). Using a variety of data sources they were able to show how changes to the organization of daily life in the post-war period might have contributed to rises in such predatory crimes. In crime terms, the massive expansion in the availability and spread of consumer durables in this period might be viewed fairly straightforwardly as a substantial rise in 'suitable targets'. In the mid-1970s FBI data suggested that nearly 70 per cent of all thefts were of/from automobiles or bicycles. In short, items that were not nearly so widely available thirty years previously. Moreover, not only were many of these items highly desirable, they were also, at least relatively speaking, portable.

The routine activities approach also suggests that the likelihood of experiencing predatory victimization is linked to elements of one's daily life. To what extent is one surrounded by 'capable guardians' during daily activities? The routine activities approach hypothesizes that those who spend more time with family, for example, are less at risk of predatory victimization than those who spend more time away from home or away from family or other primary groups. At a societal level they argue that, in the period after the Second World War, the United States saw a dramatic increase away from household-based activities toward non-household and non-family-centred activities. The nature of the labour market changed, for example, with women going out to work in significantly larger numbers, and also attending college or university on a scale quite different from pre-war levels. Attending college or going to work led to very significant increases in the purchase of cars, or 'suitable targets' as we might now think of them in this context. Work and travel also often involved the purchase of other consumer durables that might be taken and used away from home—where they were more vulnerable. Women's entry into the labour market in large numbers also reduced the numbers of people at home during the day and available to act as 'capable guardians' in local neighbourhoods.

As should by now be clear, the routine activities model also suggests that these various factors—increases in suitable targets, decreasing availability of capable guardians—may act upon each other in a way that multiply crime chances. Now, to repeat the point made earlier, Cohen and Felson were not offering anything approaching a full explanation for rising crime in the post-war period. But what their work so helpfully does is remind us that there are aspects of everyday life that offer opportunities for crime, and that these elements of daily life are not stable. They may change in ways that invite more (or less, of course) criminal activity and, in the case of the post-war period, it is precisely such changes that might help us to understand at least a significant element of the crime rise. Consequently, they observe, 'It is ironic that the very factors which increase the opportunity to enjoy the benefits of life also may increase the opportunity for predatory violations'. Just as the motor car offers freedom of movement, and involvement in college, female labour force participation, and greater access to holidays and travel all offer escape from the household, they also increase the risks of predatory crime. The routine activities approach, at heart, focuses on criminal opportunities and the risks involved in exploiting those opportunities. It has little to say about human motivation beyond suggesting that we all engage in some form of risk versus rewards calculation.

Those concerned with issues of political economy, however, would wish to see Cohen and Felson's arguments placed in a somewhat broader perspective. This would point to the massive changes in the industrial and manufacturing capabilities of many Western nations, and the huge consequences for employment, income, and general economic security that such changes meant for those working in low- and semi-skilled jobs. The associated political changes that encouraged greater individualism, privatization, and resort to the marketplace, and sought to set ever-greater limits on welfare spending, led to growing economic and social inequality from at least the late 1970s onward. In short, such a perspective would locate any opportunity-based theory within a broader account in which the changed political and economic circumstances served to remove many of the legitimate opportunities for personal gain that had previously existed while simultaneously undermining many of the community-based forms of solidarity and control that helped in the maintenance of order and control.

What if we also take a longer term perspective? Looking historically, and much influenced by the German sociologist, Norbert Elias's theory of the 'Civilizing Process', the psychologist, Stephen Pinker, argues that what happened in the decades from the 1960s to the 1980s was actually the reversal of a long-term historical trend. He argues that the best historical analyses seem to suggest that homicide rates had been in decline since the 13th or 14th centuries. Homicide here is used as a proxy for broader crime trends as the data are better: murder being more commonly reported and recorded than other crimes, even other violent crimes. Why would crime generally, and homicide more particularly, have risen during these decades? According to Pinker these trends are an indicator of a 'decivilizing trend', a reversal—and possibly only a brief reversal—of the longer term civilizing process. Elias, the originator of this theory, had argued that the process of the formation of modern nation states brought with it changes in the relationships between people within social hierarchies involving, among other things, the gradual trickling down of particular social mores and expectations. In short, over the course of centuries growing interdependence brought with it greater constraints on impulsive forms of behaviour and aggression and this led to a general tightening of social pressures toward self-control. The consequence, over this extended period was gradually increasing sensitivity towards suffering in its varying forms, and a decreasing tolerance of violence and violent displays. The best historical data that we have, courtesy of criminologists such as Manuel Eisner, is utilized by various commentators, including Pinker, to illustrate precisely such a long-term decline in violent conduct. It is this that seems to have gone into reverse since the 1960s.

Now, while the state hadn't suddenly been undermined from the 1960s onward, according to Pinker two other pillars of Elias's theory had gone somewhat into reverse. Social solidarity was being affected by a variety of forces as was the pressure to exert self-control, to conform. In this he points in particular to the emergence of youth culture, underpinned by the spread of television and radio, changes in the opportunity structures for the young, women, and the working classes, that stimulated a partial rejection of some elements of authority, disrupting some social bonds, and loosening many ties of informal social control. In short, processes of informalization and de-subordination—giving a sense of freedom from traditional constraints—are what he suggests underpins the upward trend in crime during the decades of the so-called 'permissive era'—and beyond. Now, in arguing this, Pinker is not terribly far from some of the analyses offered by those on the right of the political spectrum, such as the US commentator Charles Murray, who focused on the rise of the so-called 'underclass' in the US and Britain, and laid the blame for the crime rise at the door of the post-war welfare state. This, Murray and others' argument went, helped to undermine traditional social structures like marriage and the family, and weakened traditional social values like respect, hard work, and discipline.

Whether it is in the slightly more progressive form of Stephen Pinker, or the more conservative shape of Charles Murray, these explanations arguably underplay the structural socio-economic shifts outlined above, and place far too great an emphasis on *cultural* and *moral* change. As a consequence, they also struggle slightly to deal with what appears to have a rather sudden shift of direction in crime trends somewhere around the late 1980s/ early 1990s. Why, rather without warning so far as the bulk of criminologists were concerned, should crime have started and then continued to decline? It has taken a while, but the puzzle has recently become the centre of attention for a growing group of scholars, and it is to this we turn our attention next.

Chapter 6
Understanding the crime drop

Information from a wide variety of sources shows that crime has fallen in a large number of countries over the past twenty years or more. The NCVS suggests that violent crime in the US fell by around 70 per cent between 1993 and 2011, burglary fell by over half, and theft by over 40 per cent. Similar trends have been detected in Canada and in England and Wales, and apparently in Australia and New Zealand. A wider comparison, made possible by the International Crime Victim Survey, suggests that countries such as France, the Netherlands, and Finland have also experienced substantial crime drops. Though, as Chapter 5 indicated, assessing crime trends is fraught with difficulties, one very careful review of evidence nevertheless concluded that 'it is reasonable to refer to a general *crime drop* in Europe'. So, the trend being discussed is not one that appears to have been confined to particular cities or particular countries. Nor is it a short-term blip, but has been sustained over a significant period of time, even during periods of great economic turbulence. So how might it be explained?

The economy

Although there is now a pretty sizeable literature on the links between prevailing economic conditions and crime, what one quickly discovers is that the relationships between income, wealth, inequality, crime, and victimization, though showing some fairly clear patterns, are far from straightforward. Take burglary. Domestic burglary rates are substantially higher in poorer communities, but at the national level, overall rates of burglary tend to increase as general wealth increases, as measured by gross domestic product (GDP). Why might this be the case? The simplest answer to this conundrum is most likely that at the national level a measure like GDP is broadly indicative of the level of criminal *opportunities* (how much there is of value to steal), whereas at the household level, patterns of burglary are determined by other factors including the proximity of people with the *motivation* to want to steal, and the presence or absence of basic security measures.

In early work on economic indicators and crime, criminologists tended to look at the impact of unemployment: were rises and falls in the numbers out of work linked to trends in crime? As a result of both a lack of a clear message from such studies and increasing doubts about unemployment data, researchers began to consider the relationship between macroeconomic changes and crime levels in a variety of different ways. Studies in this vein have found that the strong economy in the United States in the 1990s reduced the number of property crimes in that period. Complicating the picture somewhat, there is some evidence of a relationship between short-term changes in property crime levels and consumption, rates of property crime growth being closely linked to economic growth. More particularly, when overall consumption grows quickly, property crime growth tends to slow down or reverse, fewer people being motivated to steal, with property crime rates tending to rise during economic recessions. Despite this apparent relationship, criminological research to date suggests that there is no simple link between broad economic change and crime levels over the long-term.

There are now a substantial number of studies examining the relationship between economic factors and the recent declines in crime, the bulk of which point to generally small effects. A study by New York University's Brennan Center, for example, estimated that increases in income in the 1990s and 2000s may have accounted for between 5 and 10 per cent of the crime drop, and that the decrease in unemployment in the 1990s was responsible for up to a further 2 per cent of that decade's crime decline. Others offer a similar picture. Though few of these focus specifically on the financial crisis of the past decade, it appears the case that the very substantial declines in crime that have been underway for at least two decades have not been reversed by the financial crisis of recent times and there seems no obvious—or simple—economic explanation for the crime drop.

However, arguably, the key word here is *simple*. Why might we imagine that something undoubtedly as complex as a long-term shift in levels of crime could be explained by something as relatively straightforward as consumer confidence, levels of unemployment, or rates of inflation? Such things may have an effect and, as outlined, there is research that suggests that they do. But as an increasing number of commentators are arguing one surely has to place such narrow economic factors in a broader context? This means a return to the study of political economy—the multi-disciplinary study of the interrelationship between politics, public policy, and economics—and examining the ways in which the operation of capitalist economic systems and their relationship with social and political policies and practices combine to shape the social world in which we live, including levels of crime.

Punishment

Politicians in particular are often keen to claim that the answer to crime is punishment. If we punish more (either by punishing a greater number of people or by punishing individual offenders more harshly, or both) this will necessarily have an impact on crime. The first question—and one we return to in Chapter 7—is

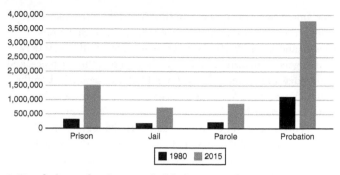

6. Population under the control of the US corrections system, 1980 and 2015.

have we been punishing more? The answer, though there are exceptions, is undoubtedly *yes*. The most obvious illustration of this is America.

Figure 6 shows the change in what is referred to as the 'correctional system' of the United States in the three and a half decades between 1980 and 2015. The US has both federal and state prisons, as well as local jails (together representing the total imprisoned population), plus those currently on parole (and thus being supervised in some form having been released from prison) or on probation. In those three decades, the prison population rose by 377 per cent, the jail population by 299 per cent, those on parole by 294 per cent, and those on probation by 239 per cent. Overall the correctional population of the United States rose almost threefold (275 per cent) to just under seven million people—equivalent to about one in thirty-six of the total adult population. So, yes, by any measure Americans are doing punishment differently. No other nation on earth imprisons such a large proportion of its population as does America, but a great many countries have gone down the route of vastly increased levels of incarceration during the period immediately preceding, as well as during, the crime drop.

How might this explain the crime decline? Most obviously there is 'deterrence'. This criminologists divide into two categories: *general* and *individual* (or *specific*) deterrence. Both are as they sound: general deterrence refers to the idea that the existence, and knowledge, of a system of punishment has a general effect on the population at large. We know that we stand a chance of being caught and punished if we break the law and, for many of us, this is enough to deter us from so doing. Individual (or specific) deterrence refers to the impact of punishment on the individual. Having been fined, put on probation, sent to prison, etc., one is deterred from committing future acts.

These ideas are both plausible and tend to become part of our general understanding of the world from quite an early age. Unfortunately, the research evidence to support such ideas is far from strong. What it shows, first of all, is that most of us respond moderately well to general threats for the more 'minor' things. So, for example, illegal parking, speeding, or littering are all examples of behaviours where there is some evidence that an increase in either the likelihood of apprehension or the severity of punishment, if one is caught, tends to affect the likelihood of doing such things. Where other crimes are concerned—everything from drug selling to violence—the evidence for the effect of deterrence is not at all strong. Why? Well many such crimes are committed away from the public gaze—there is no 'capable guardian'. Sometimes they may be carried out while under the influence of drink or drugs, or in the heat of the moment. In short, they may be less calculated and less obviously instrumental than some of those other behaviours mentioned earlier.

This is not to say that such behaviour can't be influenced, merely that the threat of punishment may not be the most effective in doing so. In fact, the research evidence suggests that it is the *certainty* of punishment that has the greatest effect. More precisely, given that being punished is dependent on being arrested, prosecuted, and convicted this finding has to be broken down further. In fact, research suggests that it is the probability of apprehension that has the greatest impact—we are more concerned about getting caught than we are about how much punishment will follow, and we are anyway generally ignorant of how the courts behave when sentencing. The reality is that most of us do not offend most of the time, but the fact that we are generally law abiding has little to do with deterrence and much more to do with what we generally refer to as 'informal social control'—in essence the influence that family, friends, and the wider community have on our behaviour (see Chapter 7).

What about individual deterrence? Surely, punishment must have an impact on the individual who is punished? Well, it does, but quite possibly less than you'd think. We generally measure the impact of punishment using what are called 'recidivism rates' or 'reconviction rates'. In the former the measure generally refers to the proportion of offenders who are re-arrested two or three years after the end of their punishment (prison, probation, etc.); the latter refers to the proportion not just arrested, but who are reconvicted after a similar period. The figures do not make happy reading.

In the United States, a study by the Bureau of Justice, which tracked over 400,000 prisoners released from state prisons during 2005, found that at the end of a five-year follow up period a staggering 78 per cent of males and 68 per cent of females had had at least one further arrest. The same study found that of all those prisoners released in one year, very nearly half (47 per cent) were re-convicted within three years. The reconviction rates ranged from 40 to 42 per cent for violent and public order offenders, to 47 per cent for drug offenders, and 53 per cent for property offenders. Moreover, the study found that over half (52 per cent) of prisoners were returned to prison within three years either because of new offending or because they were in violation of their parole. None of this, of course, is to suggest that punishment is without impact, merely that its 'success' as measured by its effect on the likelihood of future offending is not high. And this is before we begin to think about the costs—personal, social, and financial—and the possibility that punishment might itself be criminogenic.

For those imagining that punishment and, more particularly, the massive expansion in the use of imprisonment, has been the key to the declining crime rate, the research evidence on deterrence offers little comfort. Another idea favoured by those arguing for greater use of imprisonment is *incapacitation*. This is the suggestion that by removing someone from society one prevents them from committing crimes for the period of their incarceration. In principle, so the assumption goes, if we imprison the most prolific offenders for long enough, this will undoubtedly reduce the crime rate. It was captured in simple form by US President Gerald Ford in 1975 when he said:

> The crime rate will go down if persons who habitually commit most of the predatory crimes are kept in prison for a reasonable period...because they will not then be free to commit more crimes...one obvious effect of prison is to separate law breakers from the law-abiding society.

While superficially this has some attraction to it as an idea, there are a number of issues that need to be clarified. First, we have to accept that just because someone is in prison does not mean they can't commit 'crimes'. They may assault staff or other inmates—and often do—and they can, and many will, use illegal substances. Moreover, it is hardly unknown for some offenders to manage to continue their outside criminal enterprises while serving prison sentences. In just one of the many examples in his book on US prison gangs, David Skarbek describes the activities of the Mexican Mafia prison gang in California, which included the distribution of narcotics, armed robbery, and murder. They are far from alone in the US prison system.

Second, the idea of an incapacitative effect rests on the assumption that all those imprisoned would have carried on offending had they remained free to do so. Though this may be true for many it is not true for all, and consequently the assessment of any incapacitative effect needs to take this into account. Third, offenders commit crimes at very different rates and over different periods of time. If they are prolific offenders and are imprisoned at the height of their criminal 'career' then, in principle, many crimes may be prevented. If, by contrast, they are only occasional offenders, or if they are nearing the end of what would have been their 'career' in crime, then far fewer crimes will be prevented. Fourth, there is the question of sentence length. Looking at *average* sentence lengths imposed on offenders is often misleading. In England and Wales, for example, in 2016 the average sentence length was a little over sixteen months, four months longer than the average ten years earlier. What this disguises, however, is the very high turnover of prisoners on relatively short sentences. In 2016, very nearly half (47 per cent) of all those entering prison were serving a sentence of six months or less. The time served for those offenders will be considerably shorter, and the incapacitative potential of the sentence similarly limited.

Fifth, there are what are called 'substitution effects'. What if crimes are committed in groups? Perhaps a group of three burglars are operating. One is caught and imprisoned. What will the impact be? Will it stop the burglaries altogether because the imprisoned person was the ringleader? Will it reduce the burglaries by a third? Or, will it have no effect because the other two will carry on regardless or will simply recruit another to join their group? What about drug sales? At the height of the 'war on drugs' in the 1990s, David Simon, the creator of HBO's *The Wire*, wrote that the city of Baltimore's drug arrests were three times the rate of cities of comparable size, and that this had no discernible impact on local drugs markets. Finally, what if the cure is, at least in part, the cause of the illness? Can imprisonment be *criminogenic*—the cause of offending? Perhaps, as one British government document once put it, prison is simply an expensive way of making bad people worse, by keeping them in close proximity to other, perhaps more experienced, offenders; as a consequence of the brutalizing conditions in some prisons; or by diminishing their chances of employment on release among other possibilities? The research evidence offers at least some limited support for this argument. One carefully conducted Australian study of re-offending, for example, found that there was no deterrent effect in respect of some offences but, worse still, in cases such as non-aggravated assault, imprisonment actually increased the likelihood of future offending.

Although in very recent times the vast costs of imprisonment have begun to persuade some that a new approach is needed, in the main few of the cautions about the limitations of the deterrent or incapacitative effects of imprisonment appear to have had any appreciable impact on politicians or policy makers. Quite the reverse. In many countries, the US most egregiously, enormous amounts of money have been dedicated to expanding the use of imprisonment. Surely, the extraordinary increase in the numbers incarcerated in the US since 1980 must have had some impact on the crime rate? The straightforward answer is that, yes, it has. The more difficult matter to resolve is how much?

The economist, Steven Levitt, has suggested that the massive expansion in incarceration might account for as much (or *as little*, depending on your viewpoint) as one-third of the observed decline in crime in the past twenty-five years. Other estimates vary quite widely, from about 10 to 27 per cent of the crime drop. Even here we have to be careful for, as has been widely noted, the crime decline experienced by Canada—at roughly the same time as that in the US—occurred without any significant increase in incarceration. But the idea that there is any straightforward relationship between crime rates and imprisonment can be illustrated by comparing the experience of different American states. New York and Florida, for example, experienced very similar drops in recorded crime but one has seen a drop in imprisonment (by a quarter), the other a rise

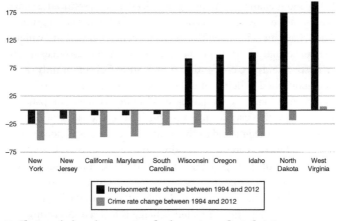

7. Changes in imprisonment and crime rates, selected states, USA, 1994–2012.

of a third. Connecticut and Idaho both had crime drops by just under a half. In the same period Connecticut's prison population increased by 5 per cent, Idaho's by over 100 per cent (see Figure 7). Punishment may have played some part in the crime drop, but we clearly need to look elsewhere for a full explanation.

Policing

There are two broad ways in which changes in policing might affect crime rates: increases in the number of police officers and changes in the ways in which the police operate. In relation to the first possibility, we now have quite a number of studies, of different designs, exploring this matter. The results? First, although it seems that increases in officer numbers may lead to declines in property crime, it is very difficult to find consistent evidence of a similar relationship between officer numbers and violent crime. Nevertheless, some of the more reliable commentators in this field are fairly sceptical about the likelihood that police numbers have played an important in the crime drop.

What about changes to policing practices? Again, some cities have seen some very substantial changes in which the police operate. These have included such things as 'hot spots policing'—in which the police analyse crime problems and focus their resources where crime problems are concentrated—the spread of community or neighbourhood policing, and the introduction of a system of management and accountability within forces, called Compstat in the US, which uses local crime data both as the basis for the analysis of problems and as the means of holding local police commanders to account for tackling those problems. Systematic analysis of 'hot spots policing' suggests that organized well it does indeed lead to *modest* decreases in crime, and that some of these benefits diffuse into areas immediately adjacent to the high crime areas where such targeted policing is focused. According to one set of calculations, the focusing of police activities using 'Compstat'-style forms of management may have contributed between 5 and 15 per cent to the crime decline where it has been used, though there are few commentators that appear to believe the scale of its impact was that significant.

One of the real difficulties faced by those hoping to link policing practices to the crime decline is that such practices vary greatly city to city and jurisdiction to jurisdiction, and yet the crime decline has been close to universal. Although policing cannot explain the overall US crime decline, one criminologist in particular has argued that policing may have had a very particular impact in New York City. A city famous for many things: its yellow cabs, its skyline, and, historically, its crime levels. In recent times, however, something quite remarkable has happened. Crime, which declined in all major American cities, declined more—often very substantially more—in New York City. Moreover, New York City's crime decline went on for longer than most other cities. Though the general crime drop in the US may have multiple causes, US criminologist, Frank Zimring, argues that New York's *extra* decline is quite possibly the result of changes in policing (see Figure 8).

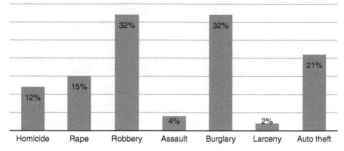

8. Estimated police crime reduction in New York City, 1990–2009.

So, what changed? One element was the number of street police from the early 1990s, where New York's police officer numbers far outstripped any other major city, and where a very significant proportion were involved in visible and targeted patrol work. The New York Police Department (NYPD) also utilized both the previously mentioned 'hot spots' and the Compstat initatives, focused particular attention on the destruction of public drug markets, and used a particularly aggressive programme of street stops and misdemeanour arrests. This leads Zimring to conclude that 'police matter' and 'they should be concentrated in the areas where the priority crimes are the heaviest'. How much difference did the NYPD make? According to Zimring policing initiatives are arguably the *only* thing that helps account for *the difference* in the crime drop between New York and other major American cities—though the security consequences of changes in routine activities in a high crime city would be at least one other possibility.

Security and prevention

For much of the 20th century political and policy attention regarding crime tended to focus on ways of intervening in the lives of offenders in order to reform or rehabilitate them. Such efforts brought mixed results. As crime increased year on year in the

1960s and 1970s a degree of disillusionment about such reform efforts set in. An influential 1974 review by the American sociologist, Robert Martinson, entitled 'What Works? Questions and Answers about Prison Reform', famously concluded, 'with few and isolated exceptions, the rehabilitative efforts that have been reported so far have had no appreciable effect on recidivism'. Such disappointing results ushered in a period in which rather than 'what works?', Martinson's work became associated with the idea that 'nothing works'.

Since that time, one significant strand of criminological attention has focused on what is referred to as 'situational crime prevention'—generally by finding ways of making the commission of crime either more difficult or less attractive. We will look at crime prevention in much more detail in Chapter 8. One of the more obviously shared characteristics of that wide range of countries that have experienced substantial crime declines is that they have all invested significantly in security provision in a number of aspects of daily life and so successful have these strategies been, goes the argument, that they have contributed very substantially to the crime drop.

The decline in car crime is often used as one of the key illustrations of the security hypothesis. The theft of motor vehicles in the US fell by 60 per cent in the ten years from 1991. Though it occurred just a few years later a very similar drop in car theft occurred in England and Wales and, though later still, the same type of crime declined by 55 per cent between 2001 and 2007 in Australia. During these periods, a variety of security technologies became widespread. In England and Wales, for example, the proportion of cars with central locking grew from 35 per cent in 1991 to almost 90 per cent by 2007. Over the same period, the proportion of cars with electronic immobilizers increased from 45 to 69 per cent. A wide range of other security devices also became available and relatively common. The increasing average

age of stolen cars offers clear evidence of the impact of security measures—older cars without security devices have become increasingly attractive to thieves, as newer cars have become increasingly difficult to steal. Similarly, evidence from both Australia and England and Wales suggests that the forcing of locks was the mode of entry that declined most significantly, this being one of the areas of car security that was quickly improved as the emphasis on crime prevention measures grew.

The next question is whether this general trend applies to other sorts of crime. Certainly, there are good reasons to believe that rates of burglary have most likely been affected by similar security shifts. Those advancing this 'security hypothesis' argue that it potentially has an even greater reach than so far suggested. They argue that crimes like car crime and burglary are both what they would call 'debut crimes'. They are things that are committed by relative novices to criminal activity. Reducing such crime, it is speculated, may thus stop offenders moving on to other forms of crime. In addition, not only is it a debut crime, but it also potentially facilitates other forms of crime—making offenders more mobile, allowing them to move stolen goods, to escape quickly from violent or other types of acquisitive crime. As a 'keystone crime' its prevention potentially leads to the prevention of other criminal acts.

There is much more research needed in this particular field, but it seems eminently plausible that security developments have been crucial to the declines of certain types of crime, and have contributed—most likely significantly, though we have no estimates—to the crime drop overall. Before we conclude, we have two further candidates to consider: the impact of abortion law reform and changes consequent on declining emissions from petrol/gas as a result of the removal of lead. Neither seem the most likely explanations perhaps, but both have generated a lot of publicity in recent years.

Abortion law reform

The first of these arguments, put forward by the journalist and economist partnership of John Donohue and Steven Levitt, suggests that the decision by the US Supreme Court in 1973 in the landmark *Roe v. Wade* case which legalized abortion is linked to the crime decline. Donohue and Levitt argue that those most likely to take advantage of this new freedom were those who were most at risk of giving birth to children who would go on to engage in crime: teenagers, unmarried women, and the most economically disadvantaged. One would therefore expect that one of the results of an increase in abortion would be a declining number of births of children with a disproportionately high likelihood of engaging in crime later in life. They then move on to show that the crime downturn occurred eighteen to nineteen years after the *Roe v. Wade* decision, a period they say is roughly in line with the peak age for violent offending or, to follow their argument, the time that the first cohort born after the change in the abortion law would have hit this peak. That crime continues to decline from this point onward is an indicator, they argue, of the continuing impact of the absence of new cohorts reaching the peak age of offending.

Reaction to this argument has often been dismissive, though it has also been subject to occasionally serious academic scrutiny. A number of fairly far-reaching criticisms have been raised. Serious doubt has been cast on whether the *Roe v. Wade* decision really had any substantial impact on births with significant risk markers (such as single mothers and teenage mothers). There is good evidence to show that the numbers of births to single mothers, for example, continued to increase through the 1970s. Nor does the evidence support the idea of a decrease in the numbers of children born into poverty. But, at least as crushingly for this theory, data from other parts of the world don't tend to support it either. Abortion law reform occurred in 1967 in England and Wales, five years before *Roe v. Wade*, and yet the crime drop arguably began around 1994/5, a few years after that in the US and when any 'first cohort' would have been almost 30 years old, way beyond any peak age of offending. Moreover, although it appears that rates of abortion were roughly similar in England and Wales and America, crime reductions—certainly so far as homicide was concerned—were much less steep in England and Wales. Again, none of this is to discount entirely the idea that abortion law reform may have had an impact, simply that there are good reasons to believe that any effect was in all likelihood considerably smaller than is sometimes claimed.

Lead in petrol

Bearing in mind that none of these factors are mutually exclusive, the final possibility I want briefly to consider has only really emerged in recent years. At heart the idea is quite simple and it concerns lead poisoning. Early in the 20th century the addition of tetraethyl lead to gasoline began to increase the efficiency of car engines very significantly. Unfortunately, though the extent of this was only discovered much later, it was also toxic and once absorbed into bones and blood could cause kidney damage, heart disease, and a variety of other problems. Increasing awareness of these problems resulted in governments moving to remove lead almost entirely from gasoline/petrol in the period between the mid-1970s and mid-1980s.

Research has shown that exposure to lead in childhood is strongly linked to a variety of behavioural traits including impulsivity, aggression, and low intelligence quotient (IQ). As mentioned earlier, all of these are key risk factors for crime. That is they are associated, especially when found in combination, with a heightened likelihood that the individual concerned will become involved in criminal activity. The suggestion, therefore, is that children born in the 1980s, who had much less exposure to lead than earlier generations have been much less likely to commit crimes when they became adults in the late 1990s and early 2000s. What is really intriguing about the lead poisoning theory is that, if one accepts the general logic of it, then not only does it help begin to explain why crime might have started to decline in the 1990s, but it would also contribute to our understanding of the massive growth in crime in the post-war period—exactly paralleling the growth in the numbers of cars on the road and the amount of lead infused fuel being consumed. How strong is the evidence for this theory?

There is a growing body of work that seems to show some quite close parallels in patterns of lead emissions in the atmosphere, and rising and declining levels of crime. Moreover, much of this work is cross-national showing that countries as widespread as the US, France, Germany, and Italy appear to show a clear pattern linking levels of lead emissions with crime trends. But there are a number of problems. Assuming the removal of lead had the effects claimed for it, the benefit would be time limited. Crime would decline as a new generation no longer affected by lead poisoning grew to maturity. But given the age-crime curve, this impact would be at its highest when they were in their peak years of offending. It would decline thereafter naturally. Thus any further crime decline—which it appears we are still experiencing—would not be explained by the fact that petrol/gasoline was less toxic. Second, epidemiological studies have not tended to find much in the way of differences between blood lead levels in groups of offenders and non-offenders, certainly not enough to explain more than a very small element of any variation. Moreover, studies have tended to be able to link declining lead emissions more easily to trends in violent crime than property crime. Indeed, a recent study in Australia shows very little support for the thesis overall. Lead levels dropped from the late 1970s onward, but the main property crime types didn't begin to fall until the early 2000s—again when those affected would be in their late 20s/early 30s and way beyond any peak age of offending. The authors admit that it is possible that declining atmospheric lead levels might have had some impact on falls in assault rates, but find little evidence for any significant link with property crime.

Final thoughts

What are we to make of all this? Well, first it does seem that there is a broad consensus that crime rose, and rose steeply, in the period after the Second World War, increasingly steeply from the 1960s onward, reaching a peak somewhere in the late 1980s or 1990s, and declining thereafter. Second, and I don't think we should be the slightest bit surprised about this, there is no simple explanation for either the *rise* or the *fall* in crime. A combination of factors, which include matters of political economy, social inequality, changes in our routine activities, and, more recently, greater attention given to security and crime prevention, most likely offer us the most coherent set of explanatory variables in unpicking the trends we have observed.

But before we finish there is one further thing we need to consider: the Internet. Perhaps there is another aspect of changes in our routine activities that we haven't yet fully taken into account—and this is that our lives, and young people's in particular, are now very differently organized than they used to be, with the consequence that they spend far less time out on the streets or in other spaces where they might get involved in the sorts of activities that traditionally are the focus of police attention. That is not to say that these young people are not involved in *crime*, for the Internet offers many other opportunities for criminal activity. It is merely that these activities are not formally policed in the same way as young people's street activities are policed.

But this last point leads on to a much more serious matter. If it is true to say that there is a certain amount of crime committed using modern information communication technologies (ICTs)—the

Internet most obviously—and it is also true to say that these matters are much less formally regulated than our traditional conceptions of crime, then perhaps our main measures of crime have underestimated just how much crime is taking place. Perhaps the crime drop has not been quite as significant as we have thought?

Luckily, the Crime Survey for England and Wales has just started playing catch up on this matter. Since 2014, it has been trying to measure fraud and cybercrime more accurately. In the year ending September 2016 the CSEW estimated that there were 6.2 million incidents of crime, down from the peak of nineteen million in the mid-1990s. However, with new experimental questions added for the first time, it also estimated an additional 3.6 million crimes of fraud and two million computer misuse offences. Adding these to headline estimate of 6.2 million crimes almost doubled it to 11.8 million. Still significantly lower than the mid-1990s peak, but in some respects a rather less substantial crime drop than we might have been assuming. Now we need many more years of such survey questions being asked, supported by much more research on the impact of the Internet on crime, before we can feel at all confident about where we stand. It is quite likely that we have indeed been experiencing a crime drop in the last twenty years, but it also seems fairly certain that even our most sophisticated measures have overestimated the extent of this drop. As we said at the end of Chapter 5, where statistics are concerned, and crime statistics more particularly, a cautious scepticism is always a healthy starting point.

Chapter 7
How do we control crime?

In this chapter, I want to discuss both the formal and less formal means that might be thought to control crime. First is to consider formal means, by and large by using what we refer to as the criminal justice system. In saying this we must recognize, of course, that our penal system has many functions beyond controlling crime, not the least of which is administering justice irrespective of its impact on offending. Second, and arising from what we know to be the limitations of organized criminal justice in relation to crime control, I want to consider the less formalized means by which crime might be held in check—the processes of socialization and learning of social norms and values, reinforced by what is often referred to as informal social control. Let's begin by looking at recent trends in the use of punishment—using examples from around the globe.

Trends in punishment

There are a variety of institutions that we now most closely associate with formal criminal justice—the police, criminal courts, and prisons being the most obvious. Most, in the main, are relatively recent arrivals. Formally organized and state funded police forces have been with us for no longer than two centuries. Prisons, though they have been around a fair while longer, in many respects differ considerably in form and function from the prisons of 200–300 years ago. The same is broadly true of the courts. Such systems are not only a modern creation, their nature and operation changes over time, and they also vary considerably from place to place.

Our systems of punishment have changed radically also. In many jurisdictions up until at least the 18th century the death penalty was a regularly used and centrally important form of punishment by the state. Though a few dozen countries retain the death penalty, including China (by far the greatest user of capital punishment), India, Japan, Singapore—and—America, it appears to be something that is slowly disappearing. The prison now generally represents the most serious penalty most states can impose. The last century or so has seen the emergence of a range of other punishments, from financial penalties such as fines or compensation to victims, through community-based sanctions such as probation, community service-style penalties, and so forth.

How has the use of punishment changed in the past half century or thereabouts? As we saw in Chapter 4, in many countries crime rates rose, often quite steeply, in the post-war years, until the late 1980s/early to mid-1990s, and then they began to fall and seemingly to fall quite dramatically. Might we expect our use of punishment to follow these trends in some way—perhaps to increase and expand as crime rises and then subsequently to fall? Such assumptions are superficially plausible but are not supported by evidence. As we saw in Chapter 6, while it would be stretching a point to suggest that there is *no* relationship between crime and punishment, it is not necessarily the one we might expect.

Let us start with the United States. As we saw in Chapter 6, so far as imprisonment is concerned, what has happened in the United States is nothing short of extraordinary. The overall federal and state prison population increased from about 30,000 to well over a quarter of a million between 1880 and 1980—a more than eightfold expansion of the numbers of Americans incarcerated.

However, the US population also grew substantially, and therefore the change to the incarceration rate—generally assessed as the number of people incarcerated per 100,000 of population—is a better indicator. This rose from 61 per 100,000 in 1880 to 145 by 1980, an increase of 133 per cent.

It is what has happened since then that is truly remarkable. The US prison population and the incarceration rate began an astonishing rise that was to be almost continuous and was to last for the best part of three decades. From an incarceration rate of 145 per 100,000 in 1980 it reached a high of over 500 per 100,000 by around 2007–8. Where the first four-fifths of the century had seen the prison population well below quarter of a million, by the early 21st century it had reached well over 1.5 million (see Figure 9). Add local jails and by this point something over 2.2 million American citizens were in prison at any one time.

If one adds together all those under some form of criminal justice supervision in America—whether in prison, on parole having been

How do we control crime?

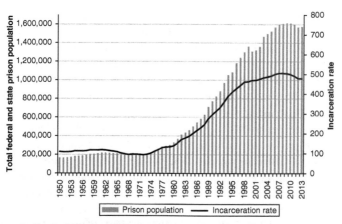

9. Federal and state prison population, and incarceration rate, USA, 1950–2013.

released from prison, or being supervised on probation in the community—the figure reached nearly 7.5 million at its peak in 2007. Put a different way, the number of people in prison, on probation, or on parole in America is roughly equivalent to the combined populations of Los Angeles and Chicago, the second and third largest cities in the country.

Once again, however, we should remind ourselves that these are very general statistics and that within America there is huge variation in the ways in which states operate their criminal justice and penal systems. Thus, for example, the correctional supervision rate—the number of people in prison, on parole, or on probation per 100,000 population—varies from just under 1,000 in the State of Maine to over 7,600 in Georgia, or one in thirteen of the adult population. As we will see, by international standards the rates of incarceration and other penal supervision even in the states with the lowest figures are extremely high. So, while we must generally guard against treating the United States crudely and uniformly, it is nevertheless the case that it stands out, comparatively, almost in whatever form it is considered.

In Australia, the growth in the prison population, and the incarceration rate, has been steady and constant. While the prison population was under 10,000 in 1982, by 2015 it had reached over 35,000, with the incarceration rate more than doubling in the same period from just under 90 per 100,000 in 1982 to almost 200 by 2015 (see Figure 10). Australia, like the US, is also a federal system and one where there are significant differences between territories. The state of Victoria, for example, had an incarceration rate of around 134 per 100,000 in 2015, whereas Western Australia's was over twice as high at 278. Both are dwarfed, however, by the prison situation in Australia's Northern Territory, which has an extraordinary incarceration rate of almost 900 per 100,000, in other words significantly higher than that of the United States (though not all individual US States). What Australia's Northern Territory shares with the US is the vastly

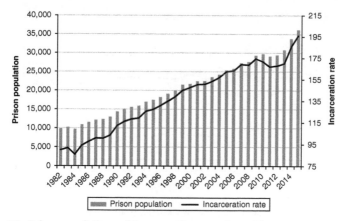

10. Prison population and incarceration rate, Australia, 1982–2015.

disproportionate representation of minorities (in this case indigenous Australians) in the prison system.

As with the US and Australia, the last twenty-five years have seen a very significant expansion in the number of people in prison in England and Wales. The prison population grew fairly steadily in the post-war years, but it was really from the early 1990s—at a point when both main political parties began to fight to be seen as tough on crime—that the most significant spurt took place.

Very much in contrast with the countries considered thus far, Canada's recent penal history has taken a different path. Both in terms of the use of prison and the use of non-custodial, community-based penalties, Canada's rates have remained relatively stable. Over a thirty-year period, Canada's incarceration rate has been all but flat (see Figure 11). At the beginning the 1980s, Canada's incarceration rate was slightly higher than that in Australia, yet by 2015 Australia's was approximately 50 per cent higher than that of Canada. Canada did experience some growth in non-custodial penalties, particularly in the late 1980s/early 1990s,

Rate per 100,000 adult population (18 years and over)

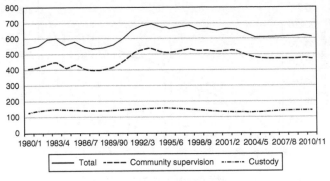

| Total | Community supervision | Custody |

11. Correctional supervision rate, Canada, 1980–2011.

but overall the correctional supervision rate (prison, probation, etc., combined) grew by less than 10 per cent between 1980 and 2011.

There are many countries that have experienced a significant shift in a punitive direction, with prison populations and incarceration rates rising, often steeply, but there are also others that buck that trend. Since the early 1990s, for example, there have been significant increases in the incarceration rates in Spain, Greece, France, Ireland, and Scotland. The Netherlands, had comparatively low levels of incarceration in the 1980s, then quadrupled its rate by 2006, before then decreasing it by almost half in the following decade. By contrast, and rather like Canada, the major Scandinavian countries—Sweden, Norway, and Denmark—have all seen relatively little change in their incarceration rates, and in Finland it has even dropped (from seventy per 100,000 in 1992 to fifty-seven in 2015).

Why is there so much variation? As we saw when discussing the crime drop in Chapter 6, there is no clear or simple relationship

Criminology

between levels and types of punishment, and crime levels. Indeed, there is now a very considerable body of research that suggests that the impact of formal criminal justice on crime rates is not necessarily all that large. This flies in the face of much public opinion, which assumes, for example, that increasing police numbers will necessarily make us safer. As we have seen, it might, but there is certainly no guarantee. The lack of any clear relationship also flies directly contrary to much political rhetoric which argues that 'tough on crime' policies—more prisons, tougher sentencing, and so on—will necessarily bring crime down. Again, it might, but as has been shown it is by much less than many would believe, and certainly less than politicians often claim. If policing, courts and prisons have a limited impact, then what else accounts for orderliness? The answer is…people in groups, small and large. We, collectively, are all engaged in an informal project which produces general social stability and order. The general predictability of life around you is a consequence, not of the presence of police officers or the threat of punishment by the courts, but, rather, is the product of the more or less predictable interactions of individuals in myriad social settings, and the internalized desire we all carry urging us to avoid the consequences that occur when such predictability is challenged. This, in general terms, is what we usually refer to as 'informal social control', the subject to which we turn next.

Socialization and informal social control

At the end of the last section, I talked of the desire most of us carry urging us to avoid the consequences that would likely result when informal expectations are not met. The American criminologist, Charles Tittle, once observed that 'social control as a general process seems to be rooted almost completely in informal sanctioning'. He went on to suggest that our perceptions of the probability or severity of formal sanctions appeared not to have much of an effect, and even where they do have an impact, much of that appears to be dependent on the way we perceive informal sanctions. When we talk of informal sanctions, what might we mean? Two examples. You're approaching someone you've met several times before; they're walking along a corridor, or a street, towards you. You can't remember their name. You know you can't avoid them, and try as you might their name just won't come into your head. Any moment you're going to have to deal with the fact that you can't easily introduce them to the person you're walking with.

Given how much difficulty many of us have with names and faces, this is a far from uncommon occurrence and most people will have experienced it. But why does it matter? It matters because of social convention. In many circumstances it is considered impolite not to introduce people who may not know each other. In short, we want to do the right thing and we fear the embarrassment of failing to abide by some essentially minor social conventions. No-one is likely to make a big deal out of it but, in ourselves, we feel a degree of discomfort—a discomfort we'd prefer to avoid. It is precisely the fact that we generally seek to avoid such discomforts in everyday life, in this case by responding to internalized informal social control stimuli, that keeps our behaviour predictable.

London's underground (subway train) system has, like most such city metro systems, a very large number of escalators, many of them quite long and steep, and, during rush hours, also very busy. The escalators are just wide enough to fit two people side by side. There is a system on the escalators in London whereby those who wish to stand still, stand on the right of the escalator, leaving a space to the left for anyone who may wish to walk. It is a largely informal system, there are no formal sanctions that can be imposed on anyone failing to conform, though there are signs on the escalators encouraging and supporting the behaviour. The system is enormously successful. By and large anyone not planning on walking up or down the escalator can always be found standing on the right, irrespective of how busy or quiet the station is. Those found static on the left are most usually visitors or others unfamiliar with the system and its informal rules—children for example. How does it work? Not through the threat of formal sanctions—there aren't any. Again, it is the power of social expectations.

Once we've learned the informal rules of the situation, most people most of the time will comply. It costs them little to do so and, crucially, they are keen to avoid the consequences of failing to comply: the unfavourable opinion of others who are unhappy that the smooth running of the escalator system has been disrupted.

Social norms and expectations frame our conduct from the moment we wake, encompassing when and how we wash and dress for example, right through the day, including when and what we eat, and the different ways in which we interact with family, friends, colleagues, and strangers. The rituals of everyday life are complicated. We have to learn and internalize them. They are rarely highly specific or inflexible, but rather are cues or broad guides about appropriate conduct. Put together, our expectations of each other and ourselves, as learned in families, schools, communities, workplaces, and so on, form the fundamental basis for the orderliness of everyday life. This is what the American sociologist, Erving Goffman, called the *interaction order*, the workings of which, he suggested, could easily be viewed as the consequences of 'systems of enabling conventions' and something like the ground rules of a game.

How do the participants in this 'game' learn its general ground rules? At heart, and put slightly differently, this simple yet profound question can be put as 'what is it that makes us *social* beings? How do we learn to behave in groups, small and large? The process is what we call *socialization*. We tend to think of the main agents of this process as being family, community, friends/peers, school, work, media, and, at least traditionally, religion. My two granddaughters visited today. The older of the two is, like all 4-year-olds, immensely energetic and in need of a lot of general supervision. Family interaction consequently involves lots of guidance about how to behave: 'please come and sit at the table to eat'; 'I think we ought to put all these games away if we're finished with them', or, on the way to local playground, 'please don't run here, it's a very busy road'. No doubt there were dozens of these, in part intended as tiny building blocks in a young person's development, and in part all helping to maintain the particular interaction order that is our family.

Parenting involves issuing regular reminders about what to do and say, about what is expected in some circumstances but not in others, and offering guidance about how different forms of conduct are likely to be understood and perceived by others. Much of this is done explicitly, though oftentimes children learn simply through interaction—learning the different responses their behaviour is likely to produce. The socialization of young children by their parents is fairly easy to understand, and in many respects the same may largely be said of the influence of the other main 'agents' of socialization. It is not hard to understand how schools, especially when children are young, play a crucial role in their moral education and development. Similarly, friendship and peer groups can exercise considerable sway over individuals and may be of very particular importance at certain stages of development. The world of work, the influence of mass media and increasingly of social media, and the role of organized religion—all of these are potentially of great significance in helping understand how what Goffman referred to as the 'enabling conventions' or ground rules of everyday conduct are learned.

Now, let us return to crime control. In the most general terms criminological thinking can be divided into two camps. First, there are those who begin from the assumption that humans are broadly compliant and orderly, and the key question therefore becomes why do they sometimes commit crimes? By contrast there are those who begin from the assumption that we are generally unruly and self-interested, and from this starting point the key question becomes what restrains us and why so much of the time do we seem to comply with rules? Crudely put, the first band of criminologists is interested in the differing motivations individuals may have for committing crimes, whereas the second are more focused on the different restraints or controls likely to be in operation. If forced to choose I would be more in the latter camp than the former but, fortunately, one doesn't have to choose, and consequently both perspectives can be utilized in attempting to understand human conduct.

The second group of criminologists would broadly fall into a camp called 'control theorists'. One of the earliest statements outlining this position came from Jackson Toby who, writing in the 1950s, focused in particular on what was at stake in rule breaking:

> the differences between the law-abiding adolescent and the hoodlum is not that one has impulses to violate the rules of society while the other has not. Both are tempted to break laws at some time or other—because laws prohibit what circumstance may make attractive: driving an automobile at 80 miles an hour, beating up an enemy, taking what one wants without paying for it. The hoodlum yields to these temptations. They boy living in a middle-class neighbourhood does not. How can this difference be accounted for?

His answer was that these two generalized individuals have different *stakes in conformity*. In short, one has much more to lose if found out than does the other. Their 'good reputation', perhaps their job, or their educational opportunities, might be jeopardized by public revelation of such infractions. The implication of the use of the term 'hoodlum' is that this individual is either known or expected to be someone who would break such social conventions. Their reputation is already compromised. Almost certainly they have less to lose in terms of education or employment. Subsequently, this position was refined with others arguing that what prevented individuals from acting on criminal

motivations was what they called a *commitment to conformity*,
or later was referred to as the *social bond*. Developed via
socialization, this could involve loss—of reputation, the good
opinion of others, self-esteem—as well as gain in the shape of
anticipated future rewards. What is being described here is a
developmental process involving the gradually increasing social
integration of the individual. Imprisonment, one might argue,
does precisely the opposite, disrupting social ties, loosening
attachments of various types, and, overall, working to reduce
the degree of social integration of the individual concerned.

The next step for control theorists is to consider the forms of
control that bear upon and constrain any deviant desires. There
are internalized controls, inhibitions resulting from moral beliefs,
conscience, or *shame*; indirect controls in the form of social
censure that comes from family members, peers, and others; and
the more direct forms of control that come from concern about
formal sanctions. Control theorists tend to argue that some
combination of indirect control, especially by the family, and
self-control that results from concern for the long-term
consequences of conduct is crucial in the process of enabling
temptation to be resisted.

From my point of view, the most sophisticated and persuasive
work in this tradition is the 'age-graded theory of informal social
control' associated with Robert Sampson and John Laub. For
these authors it is the strength of the individual's social bond that
helps explain the presence or absence of offending and, similarly,
changes in individuals' offending patterns over time reflects
changes in the strength of the social bond in their lives. Their
general thesis has three main elements. First, delinquency early
in life (childhood and adolescence) is a product of the structural
context in which young people grow up mediated by the social
controls exerted by neighbourhood, family, school, and friends.
Second, the patterns established in these early years tend to be
fairly stable, just as the control systems affecting individuals tend

to be; and, third, changing patterns of criminality over the later life course reflect the effectiveness of informal social bonds to family and employment.

In later work these authors have broadened their explanations of patterns of offending over the life course to take in such matters as personal agency and (situated) choice, routine activities, local cultures, and macro-level historical events. In focusing more particularly on local area effects—why the variations in the levels and patterns of crime in different places appear to be relatively stable—they introduce a number of other conceptual tools, such as *collective efficacy* and *community capital*. At heart, the arguments relate to the differential abilities of neighbourhoods to 'realize the common values of residents and maintain effective social controls'. In this regard, social control does not refer to formal regulation or to the 'forced conformity' induced by institutions like the police and the courts but, rather, is a more general reference to the ability of a group to regulate its members according to particular norms and values. Just as in the earlier discussion of the major influences on the patterns of offending in the lives of individuals so, here, the same general point is being made in relation to the patterning of crime within different neighbourhoods. It is *informal* rather than *formal* social control that exerts the crucial influence. Although criminologists differ in their explanations of crime and criminality, few would demur from this general observation.

How do we control crime?

A historical perspective is always important for it gives the lie to easy assumption that the way we do things now is the same or similar to the ways we've always done things. In this context it helps remind us that the formal apparatuses we have designed for dealing with crime—police, courts, prisons, and so on—are actually a largely modern product and have been in existence in their current general form for little more than two centuries.

These formal systems of justice also vary, sometimes quite considerably, according to the structure and culture of the societies in which they operate. For our purposes here, perhaps the most important lesson, and one with no little irony for the subject of criminology, is that the things that criminologists spend a very great deal of their time studying—the police, the courts system, prisons, and other institutions of formal criminal justice—are not thought to be *the* crucial determinants of the nature and level of crime.

Charles Tittle, quoted earlier, went so far as to suggest that 'it looks as if objective, formal sanctions (or provisions for such) are actually largely irrelevant to general social control, at least in the direct, immediate sense'. 'Irrelevant' may be a little on the strong side, for it would be wrong to suggest that these institutions have no effect—of course they do—and they are anyway important social institutions worthy of careful academic scrutiny. But, we should note that both historically and currently, it is arguably the case that criminologists have tended to focus less on systems of informal social control than they deserve. Arguably the priority, therefore, is to try to ensure that such processes are brought fully into the centre of criminological concerns as well as to argue in support of resources and programmes that will help to reinforce those social institutions—families, schools, neighbourhoods, work, and so forth—that play the vital roles in creating and sustaining social integration and social solidarity.

Chapter 8
How do we prevent crime?

Earlier in the book we looked at crime trends, discovered that by our main measures crime appears to have dropped since the mid-1990s, and asked how this might be explained? Predictably, we found that there were no easy or simple answers to the question. A wide variety of influences affect levels of crime. These include such matters as changes in the economy and demographic shifts, all the way through to such possibilities as rising and falling amounts of lead in the atmosphere. All of these, it should be noted, are non-criminal justice influences. Although, and very understandably, it is often assumed that the police and other parts of the criminal justice system are absolutely crucial in determining crime levels, the available evidence doesn't bear this out. In fact, as we saw in Chapter 7, it is almost certainly the case that processes of socialization underpinned and reinforced by informal social control play a vital role in controlling crime. In terms of formal interventions, as Chapter 6 indicated, there is now considerable evidence to suggest that various crime prevention techniques have contributed very substantially to recent apparent reductions in crime. Indeed, research in the broad field of crime prevention has been one of criminology's greatest contributions in recent times.

Discussions of crime prevention usually begin by drawing a distinction between what tend to be referred to as *social* and *situational* approaches. Social crime prevention tends to focus on fairly broad and deep issues—what some might think of as reasonably 'fundamental' causes of crime, addressing such things as poverty, inadequate education and socialization, poor housing, and lack of employment opportunities. Situational prevention, by contrast, is narrower in focus, is pre-emptive and seeks, through a variety of means, to reduce the opportunities for crime.

Criminologists have long been interested, though they may not have used the term, in social crime prevention. One of the very best-known, and most widely publicized, social crime prevention initiatives was something called the High/Scope Perry Pre-School Project. Based in Michigan in the US, the project, which began in the 1960s, was an intervention with a group of 'high risk' children—in essence, children displaying a significant number of the early life risk factors that research has shown are associated with future probability of criminal offending. The programme offered intensive, high quality, pre-school involvement every weekday for two years, focusing particularly on the children's intellectual and social development. A total of 127 African-American 3–4-year-olds were involved, 58 being randomly assigned to the intervention and, for comparison, a further 65 to a control group that did not go through the programme. The children were of low socio-economic status, had low IQ scores, and were very much at risk of educational failure and, of course, of future involvement in crime. The programme has become well known partly because it has been subject to well-designed evaluative research and partly because of its seemingly successful results. The two groups of matched children were followed up every year from the ages of 4 to 11, and then at 14, 15, and 19, and intermittently subsequently.

Though focused primarily on education, the programme appears to have delivered a broad range of positive outcomes.

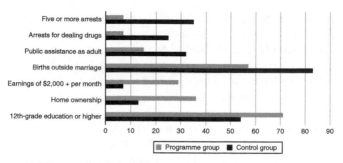

12. **Major outcomes of the High/Scope Perry Pre-School Project for participants at age 27.**

Educationally, the children involved in the programme scored higher on a number of criteria, not least their likelihood of graduating from high school. They were economically more successful, being less likely to be in receipt of public assistance, more likely to earn more and to own their own home than the children in the control group. In terms of their conduct they were less likely to have been involved in violence, had lower arrest rates, and lower contact rates with the police (see Figure 12). A cost-benefit analysis suggested that the investment in pre-school education for these children had resulted in a saving more than seven times the original cost. Researchers suggested that the return to the taxpayer from savings in welfare assistance, special education, and criminal justice was over $80,000 per child. As a consequence, the High/Scope Perry Pre-school Project is regularly used as an exemplar, illustrating the potential of social crime prevention initiatives.

The growth of interest in situational crime prevention (SCP) is a much more recent development, and reflects changes in our broader orientation towards crime and its control. When discussing trends in punishment in Chapter 7 we noted the significant shift towards increased punitiveness experienced in many Western democracies in the latter years of the 20th century.

This shift in the ways in which crime is talked about, thought about, and responded to was underpinned by a move away from some broadly held ideals that had been prominent earlier in the century. Most obviously, it involved a very significant decline in faith in what has often been referred to as the 'rehabilitative ideal'. As a young British Home Secretary in 1910, Winston Churchill famously remarked that that 'the mood and temper of the public in regard to the treatment of crime and criminals is one of the most unfailing tests of the civilization of any country'. Reflecting a very strong rehabilitative ethic, he then went on to say:

> A calm and dispassionate recognition of the rights of the accused against the State, and even of convicted criminals against the State, a constant heart-searching by all charged with the duty of punishment, a desire and eagerness to rehabilitate in the world of industry all those who have paid their dues in the hard coinage of punishment, tireless efforts towards the discovery of curative and regenerating processes, and an unfaltering faith that there is a treasure, if you can only find it, in the heart of every man—these are the symbols which in the treatment of crime and criminals mark and measure the stored-up strength of a nation, and are the sign and proof of the living virtue in it.

Until approximately the 1960s or thereabouts, such a view largely dominated professional, political, and public views about crime in many Western nations. From that point onward, fractures began to appear and subsequent decades saw this broad rehabilitative ideal gradually challenged and in some ways superseded by a number of other ideas, discourses, and practices, many of which were highly punitive in intent, outcome, or both. The decline in faith in traditional rehabilitative approaches was accompanied by increased support for greater use of, and harsher, punishments. Incapacitation grew as a justification for the use of incarceration, and the growing influence of rational choice models of human behaviour turned attention away from social influences on offending and towards concerns with individual responsibility. All of this was underpinned by very substantial changes in the politics of law and order in which—in the US and the UK, for example—there emerged a new political consensus which focused on tough rhetoric and increasingly on tough practice in the field of law and order.

In parallel with these shifts there also occurred some changes in the viewpoints of some criminologists. Increasingly dismayed by what appeared to be the disappointing impact of traditional approaches to crime and offending, some academics began to explore what they hoped would be more effective avenues. The consequence was that criminology's traditional concern with the 'deep' social causes of crime was increasingly joined, and in some ways superseded, by a more pragmatic and focused form of SCP. As I have already implied, it is no exaggeration to argue that this SCP movement has been one of the most significant criminological developments of the past half-century. In what follows we will look at the basic building blocks of SCP, consider some of the theoretical ideas that underpin it, explore one or two illustrative case studies, as well as considering some criticisms levelled at it.

Situational crime prevention

As already suggested, situational prevention focuses on the idea that crime is largely *opportunistic* behaviour. It is an approach that deliberately avoids the traditional concerns of social crime prevention such as poverty, poor housing, educational disadvantage, and so on. Rather, it has a more immediate and practical intent, focusing on measures that are targeted at specific forms of crime (rather than crime in general), which affect the management or design of the environment, and which have the aim of either making crime more risky to do or reducing its attractiveness in other ways.

One very early example of such an approach was the idea of 'defensible space', developed by the architect and city planner, Oscar Newman. In his book of the same name, Newman championed the idea of environmental design as the basis for crime prevention. Newman was critical of the design of many contemporary housing schemes arguing that they made it difficult for residents to look out for each other and to recognize strangers, that there were too many unsupervised entry and exit points making it too easy for offenders to come without notice and leave without being apprehended. He recommended increasing the opportunities for natural surveillance so that residents could see what was happening around them, using design principles to impart a sense of security, as well as adopting a variety of other measures to increase a feeling of 'territoriality'—all of which would be 'a model for residential environments which inhibits crime by creating the physical expression of a social fabric which defends itself'. Parallel theoretical developments included C. Ray Jeffrey's idea of 'crime prevention through environmental design'—which shared some of Oscar Newman's concerns but also focused on the genetic bases of offending as well as the physical environment—and Herman Goldstein's advocacy of 'problem-oriented policing' which sought to make police departments more proactive in orientation and problem-solving in approach.

Centrally, SCP argues that: opportunity plays a role in all crime; opportunities are specific, and are concentrated spatially and temporally; opportunities can be reduced; and, reducing opportunities in one place can reduce crime overall, not just *displace* it to other places. In the last three decades, SCP has become increasingly sophisticated—though some critics remain concerned about its reliance on a form of rational choice theory. The underlying assumption is that we are, as individuals, 'utility maximizers': that is to say we proceed on the basis of decisions that we hope will be of maximum benefit to us while minimizing the costs. We are mini-accountants, calculating profit and loss, and steering a course that we anticipate will serve us best.

From such a viewpoint, crimes are simply acts committed with the intention of accruing some form of benefit—broadly understood, not just monetary. The application of this form of rational choice theory leads to the further assumption that if one can tamper with the balance of benefits and costs, or risks, one should be able to change potential offenders' decision-making. A further implication is that offender decision-making is crime-specific. There are different motivations in different circumstances and, therefore, preventative efforts need to be carefully targeted. Now one might object to the idea that we are all careful decision-makers, weighing the odds and making rational decisions about courses of action. What about emotions? What about limited information, limited intelligence, pathology? The answer is to be found in the idea of 'bounded rationality'. In short, it is argued that even in circumstances where there is only fleeting consideration given to a course of action, and decisions are based on extremely limited information, there remains a degree of rationality in the process. Offenders are 'doing the best they can within the limits of time, resources and information available to them'. These mental calculations made by all offenders, even if momentary, can be exploited for crime prevention purposes.

Routine activity theory

Arguably the most influential of all the approaches within this general field of SCP is 'routine activity theory' (RAT). As we saw in Chapter 4, one of the most sophisticated uses of RAT is to be found in Lawrence Cohen and Marcus Felson's macro-level attempt to build a generalized explanation of long-term crime trends in the post-war period. Subsequently, and again associated first and foremost with the American criminologist, Marcus Felson, RAT has been used in a more immediately practical way as the basis for understanding what Felson calls the 'chemistry of crime'. This has the three components we met in Chapter 4: a motivated offender; suitable targets; and, an absence of capable guardians. First and obviously, for a crime to be committed there needs to be someone who both wants to and is capable of committing that crime—the motivated offender. Second, there must be a suitable target: something, for example, that they wish to steal or vandalize, or someone they wish to assault or defraud. The third and final element is an absence: the lack of the presence of someone or something that is capable of preventing the offence. These three things together offer the basis—the chemistry—for criminal acts. The argument in RAT is that changing any of these elements carries the potential for significant crime preventive benefits.

Of the three elements in RAT, it is the suitable target and the absence of capable guardians that tend to be the key focus of preventative activities. Offender motivation is assumed to reflect the cost-benefit calculation resulting from a comparison of the attractiveness of the target and the degree of risk involved. Capable guardians are people or things that might prevent a likely offender and a suitable target coming together in time and space. The attractiveness of a target is thought to be determined by six criteria, usually summarized by the acronym, CRAVED: referring to the extent to which a target was *Concealable*, *Removable*, *Available*, *Valuable*, *Enjoyable*, and *Disposable*.

Derek Cornish and Ron Clarke, two of the earliest advocates of SCP and of an approach to preventing crime that stresses the importance of opportunity, have identified twenty-five core approaches to crime prevention. These are represented in Table 1.

A few examples will help illustrate how SCP initiatives—as influenced by RAT—are thought to work. Those in the first column of Table 1 seek to increase the effort involved in the commission of crime. One of the most spectacular illustrations of the power of SCP is arguably the decline in vehicle crime that has occurred in the last quarter of a century and which we discussed briefly in Chapter 5. Where once relatively little

Table 1. Twenty-five techniques of situational prevention.

Increase the Effort	Increase the Risks	Reduce the Rewards	Reduce Provocations	Remove Excuses
1. Target harden: • Steering Column locks and immobilisers • Anti-robbery screens • Tamper-proof packaging	**6. Extend guardianship:** • Take routine precautions: go out in group at night, leave signs of occupancy, carry phone • 'Cocoon neighborhood watch'	**11. Conceal targets:** • Off-street parking • Gender-neutral phone directories • Unmarked bullion trucks	**16. Reduce frustrations and stress:** • Efficient queues and polite service • Expanded seating • Soothing music/muted lights	**21. Set rules:** • Rental agreements • Harassment codes • Hotel registration
2. Control access to facilities: • Entry phones • Electronic card access • Baggage screening	**7. Assist natural surveillances:** • Improved street lighting • Defensible space design • Support whistleblowers	**12. Remove targets:** • Removable car radio • Women's refuges • Pre-paid cards for pay phones	**17. Avoid disputes:** • Separate enclosures for rival football fans • Reduce crowding in pubs • Fixed cab fares	**22. Post instructions:** • 'No Parking' • 'Private Property' • 'Extinguish camp fires'
3. Screen exits: • Ticket needed for exit • Export documents • Electronic merchandise tags	**8. Reduce anonymity:** • Taxi driver IDs • 'How's my driving?' decals • School uniforms	**13. Identify property:** • Property marking • Vehicle licensing and parts marking • Cattle branding	**18. Reduce emotional arousal:** • Controls on violent pornography • Enforce good behaviour on football field • Prohibit racial slurs	**23. Alert conscience:** • Roadside speed display boards • Signatures for customs declarations • 'Shoplifting is stealing'
4. Deflect offenders: • Street closures • Separate bathrooms for women • Disperse pubs	**9. Utilize place managers:** • CCTV for double-decker buses • Two clerks for convenience stores • Reward vigilance	**14. Disrupt markets:** • Monitor pawn shops • Controls on classified ads • License street vendors	**19. Neutralize peer pressure:** • 'Idiots drink and drive' • 'It's OK to say No' • Disperse troublemarkers at school	**24. Assist compliance:** • Easy library checkout • Public lavatories • Litter bins
5. Control tools/ weapons: • 'Smart' guns • Disabling stolen cell phones • Restrict spray paint sales to juveniles	**10. Strengthen formal surveillance:** • Red light cameras • Burglar alarms • Security guards	**15. Deny benefits:** • Ink merchandise tags • Graffiti cleaning • Speed humps	**20. Discourage imitation:** • Rapid repair of vandalism • V-chips in TVs • Censor details of modus operandi	**25. Control drugs and alcohol:** • Breathalysers in pubs • Server intervention • Alcohol-free events

Source: *Theory to Practice in Situational Crime Prevention*, Crime Prevention Studies Vol. 16, edited by Martha J. Smith and Derek B. Cornish.

attention was paid by vehicle manufacturers to the problem of theft of and from vehicles, it is now effectively standard to have security devices fitted. In England and Wales, for example, where in 1991 only a third of cars had central locking, the figure had risen to 90 per cent by 2006–7. In 1991, only 23 per cent of cars had alarms. Fifteen years later the figure was over 60 per cent. In the same period car theft almost halved. Moreover, two-thirds of the decline was accounted for by temporary theft—joyriding and the taking of cars for other primarily fleeting purposes—opportunistic offences being the ones most obviously deterred. A very similar pattern has been detected in Australia, though the delayed introduction of car immobilizers there is paralleled by a later drop in vehicle-related crime. Australian research also indicates that the average age of stolen cars has been increasing—older cars being less likely to have the newer security features and therefore being those that are easier to steal.

The second strategic strand in SCP is to increase the perceived risks associated with committing crime. Here perhaps the most obvious example concerns the impact of closed-circuit television (CCTV), a relatively new technological development that will be a familiar sight to most readers—and particularly to those in Britain where CCTV is especially prevalent. One particular experiment, which took place in Chicago, Illinois, in the US, used thirty portable police operation devices—cameras that were sited in high crime neighbourhoods and which were controlled by nearby police officers who had a portable terminal in their patrol car. This allowed them to view in real time and to respond immediately where necessary. Researchers selected two areas of Chicago for study: Humboldt Park and West Garfield Park. Comparison areas with similar baseline crime patterns were also identified as a basis for evaluating the extent of any changes detected. The areas were studied over a period of five years. In Humboldt Park drug-related and robbery offences declined by around one-third, and violent crime by about one-fifth.

One possibility, of course, was that drug dealers and others had simply moved the location of their activities. Or, as the researchers would have put it, perhaps the crime had simply been *displaced*? In this case there was no evidence that this had occurred. The presence of the cameras, it seems, together with the police and prosecution activity that was linked to the recordings the cameras made, had the consequence of making some people change their conduct. In West Garfield Park, however, the outcome was different. There, after an initial fall after cameras were installed, crime actually increased, especially violent crime. It was not entirely clear to the researchers why there was such a difference between the two areas, though their hypothesis was that the police behaved differently—those in Humboldt being much more attentive to the cameras and responsive to what they saw—and that the cameras were placed in a much less concentrated fashion in West Garfield Park. Nevertheless, overall, in their cost-benefit analysis researchers estimated that the City of Chicago made savings of between $3 and $4 for every $1 spent. Research in other cities and other countries tends to reflect these general findings. We are still some way from having enough research evidence to be able to identify the optimal circumstances for the effective use of CCTV but, in summary, we know that CCTV tends to lead to modest, but far from insignificant falls in crime, and is much more effective in some places (car parks and public transport for example) than others (city and town centres).

One of the more influential developments in the field of prevention is what is known as 'hot spots policing'. This initiative arose from the observation that crime tends to be clustered spatially: some places will be much more crime prone than others. In one classic study conducted in Minneapolis in the US, researchers found that half of all calls to police came from only 3 per cent of addresses in the city. One response to this finding was to experiment with police patrol. Where once it had been thought that perhaps standard police patrol was a waste of resources—officers being most unlikely to come across a crime as it was occurring—perhaps focusing on 'hot spots' would yield a different result? Using experimental methods, the researchers were able to show a significant and sustained reduction in crime in areas where increased and targeted police patrols were undertaken—in essence placing officers where problems were concentrated.

A third approach to opportunity reduction is to reduce the anticipated rewards of crime. One of the best-known examples here concerns the successful cleaning up of New York's subway system. At one time the subway trains were covered in graffiti, and numerous attempts to solve the problem, including increasing security and using paint that was supposedly resistant to graffiti, had been tried and had failed. In the event, the answer was to tackle the graffiti artists' rewards system. What benefits did they get from such activities? Being seen was the key. Having one's 'tag' visible to others was the primary reward that was being sought and therefore being deprived of an audience became central to preventing crime. The transit authority began a policy of cleaning up the trains as soon as possible, ensuring that no trains that had been affected by graffiti were allowed back in service. The decline in graffiti, and in graffiti-related arrests was remarkable. Indeed, as two insiders involved in the programme observed, the scale of the problem had been 'considered so intractable that its eradication was considered by some to be one of the most successful urban policy "wins" on record'.

The fourth strand deals with what might be thought to be some of the everyday 'provocations' in life; for example those frustrations and stresses that can lead to conflict. Although it is accepted that it is likely fairly easy for most people to avoid such provocations most of the time, there will be some people and some particular circumstances where this is much less the case. Perhaps the clearest illustrations of the potential for preventive activity in this regard have been in the somewhat extreme environment of the prison, these being places where negative stimuli are common, experienced regularly, and not easy to avoid. Situational prevention techniques have been applied to the challenge of reducing violence between inmates, and between inmates and staff in a variety of ways, not least by reducing the frustrations associated with overcrowding and other de-humanizing elements of prison life.

The fifth set of strategies that Cornish and Clarke identify are those that attempt to remove the excuses associated with crime. In the 1950s, two American scholars, Gresham Sykes and David Matza argued very convincingly that the value systems of young delinquents were not much different from those of the adults in their communities, it was merely that they developed a series of strategies—so-called 'techniques of neutralization'—that enabled them to temporarily suspend those moral rules that would ordinarily hold criminal behaviour in check. These techniques are essentially excuses or rationalizations that help justify the acts concerned. Burglars, for example, will commonly claim that they are not really affecting anyone because surely everyone's insured anyway?

In terms of crime prevention or reduction, behavioural economists have recently shown how appealing to social norms can encourage compliance in a number of ways. Experiments in the UK, US, and Australia have shown how a simple change in the letters sent to people who have not paid their parking fines can substantially improve payment rates. In one experiment, the addition of a simple sentence to the letter received by non-payers in Kentucky, US, saying 'the majority of drivers who receive a parking fine in Louisville pay it within 13 days', together with other small changes, was found to increase repayment rates by 10 per cent. Indeed, there is an increasing body of experimental work which suggests that what is called 'behavioural norm messaging'—saying something like 'nine of ten people do [conduct concerned]' is enough to increase compliance and cooperation from citizens across a range of behaviours, from paying taxes to settling court fines, and so forth.

Repeat victimization

So far we have encountered the idea that crime is not evenly distributed in terms of *where* it takes place. In some respects this will not be an especially surprising idea to most readers, though the degree to which it is concentrated may be. Another matter, which on the surface may not seem that surprising is that criminal victimization is not evenly distributed either—of course, the fact that people live in places that are more or less crime prone than others will affect their chances of being burgled, assaulted, and so on. Moreover, people's routine activities—their lifestyles if you like—also affect the probability that they will experience crime at some point. Young men who spend part of their leisure time in pubs and clubs on Friday and Saturday nights are much more likely to become victims of violence than middle-aged people who are more circumscribed in how often and where they go out.

But one of the more important criminological findings of recent decades is the discovery, via analysis of victimization surveys, that not only are some people multiply victimized, but having been a victim of crime may actually *increase* rather than decrease the likelihood of further victimization in the future. Around 40 per cent of all crimes reported to the International Crime Victims Survey in 2000, for example, were repeat offences against targets that had already experienced at least one offence in the previous year. Although the fact that someone has recently broken into my house and stolen things might reasonably make me feel that it must be someone else's turn next time, in truth the chances of it happening again have probably increased. Why?

In relation to the example of burglary there are a number of possibilities. Burglars may return having realized that there were still goods left worth stealing or that there would be new or replacement items that could be taken. They might talk to others about the opportunities there, or the house itself might simply have characteristics that make it especially vulnerable to burglars. Moreover, there are certain types of crime where repetition is a key feature. Here, domestic violence is perhaps an obvious and very serious example. In these cases, the victim is in a relationship with a perpetrator and, in the language of RAT, by definition therefore there is almost certainly not only a motivated offender but also a 'suitable target', and most likely an absence of capable guardians (women experiencing such violence often being unwilling or unable to report, or potentially finding the police incapable of intervening, or unwilling to do so). Similar observations about risks of repeat victimization might be made about the abuse of children, and also about racist abuse and violence. Rational choice theory seems to apply particularly well to the area of repeat victimization. As one group of authors put it, 'the same or different offenders may easily take candy from a baby, until the baby runs out of candy, they grow out of wanting candy, or until a candy guardian arrives'.

Displacement and diffusion

I have already mentioned 'displacement' more than once and we should consider it a little further as it is the most often raised criticism of SCP-style initiatives. In the cases cited earlier in this chapter the issue was the potential for crime to be displaced spatially—from one place to another. However, there are a number of possibilities. Crime can also be displaced temporally (offenders changing the time at which they commit crimes), tactically (offenders changing their methods), in terms of target (offenders shifting their focus from one type of business to another, for example), and offence (offenders switching the type of crime they commit). The problem of displacement is that it raises the possibility that crime prevention measures are not really reducing crime at all, they are merely rearranging it in some way. Now,

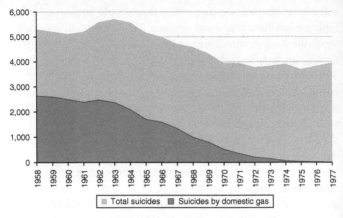

6,000
5,000
4,000
3,000
2,000
1,000
0

1958 1959 1960 1961 1962 1963 1964 1965 1966 1967 1968 1969 1970 1971 1972 1973 1974 1975 1976 1977

■ Total suicides ■ Suicides by domestic gas

13. Suicides, total and by domestic gas, England and Wales, 1958–77.

in some cases, there is undoubtedly some truth in this and considerable energy has been expended by researchers in this field attempting to estimate and assess the potential displacement effects of crime prevention efforts.

All this said, there are a good many reasons not to be too downbeat where the issue of displacement is concerned. One well-known story that is worth retelling offers very considerable hope that prevention in one place, or in one way, needn't necessarily mean problems arise elsewhere. The illustration concerns suicide, and, more particularly, what was a fairly sudden and sustained decline in the number of suicides in England and Wales between 1963 and 1975 (see Figure 13). In the early 1960s over 40 per cent of all suicides were as a result of the inhalation of domestic gas which, at that time, was highly toxic. The decline in the number of suicides—something of the order of one-third at a time when suicide was rising in many European countries—seems to have been a consequence of the progressive removal of carbon monoxide from domestic gas supplies.

This story is of particular interest here, even though it is not about crime, because the detoxification of domestic gas supplies not only caused the decline in gas suicides, but it affected overall suicide levels. Put crudely, it suggests that a sizeable number of people who might otherwise have killed themselves were prevented from doing so by the fact that they had no ready supply of poisonous gas. Crucially for our discussion here there was no major displacement; these people, it appears, did not suddenly find a new means of ending their lives. As the authors of the study put it, the gas suicide story offers clear evidence that reducing opportunities brought clear benefits that were not offset through displacement. Indeed, even if some displacement occurred, possibly as people turned to less lethal methods, thousands of lives were still saved. Clear grounds for optimism, then, where opportunity reduction is concerned.

Nevertheless, it has been suggested that practitioners have spent so much time defending their work against criticisms such as displacement, that they have paid insufficient attention to potentially more profitable lines of inquiry, including the possibility that crime prevention efforts might have benign, or even potentially positive, displacement effects. In this regard, Ken Pease, a British criminologist, argued somewhat controversially that displacement might be considered benign if, rather than reducing crime overall, it simply helped spread the risks. Moving crime around could in theory, he suggested, be broadly socially democratic in character, equalizing victimization rates, and helping to mitigate the current situation where some neighbourhoods, and some people, shoulder an unfair proportion of the burden.

In fact, once researchers started to look more closely at such ideas, they began to find that there were even more positive possibilities, including that the benefits of prevention activities in one place might be spread or diffused to others. Again, such diffusion of benefits can be seen in a number of ways, not only diffusing from target areas to neighbouring areas, but the possibility that crime types not directly addressed by prevention measures might be reduced, or that crime might reduce at times when prevention measures were not in force. Unfortunately, direct research on the diffusion of crime prevention benefits is still in its infancy. Nevertheless, the few rigorous studies that do exist have shown positive results.

One sizeable study in Jersey City, New Jersey, which focused crime prevention efforts in two areas and on two specific crime problems—street prostitution in one and drugs markets in the other—found sizeable reductions in crime in the target areas, as well as in the neighbouring areas, both immediate and some way removed, where there were no specific interventions. Part of the explanation for the fact that the prostitution problem in one area was not moved to the neighbouring areas was that these other areas did not have the vacant buildings and lack of residences of the original hot spot. In short, the potential new areas had a concentration of capable guardians which made them unattractive—riskier—spaces for the sex trade to operate in. The researchers suggested that moving criminal activities from one place to another often involves substantial effort and increased risk for offenders. Qualitative research from the same study, for example, found that those involved in the drugs trade felt that even moving a few blocks meant that they 'would have to start from scratch', that it would take time to rebuild their customer base, and that, as a consequence, the financial rewards would not be the same as previously.

In such ways crime prevention efforts directed in one place, or at one type of crime, may have unanticipated benefits elsewhere. Indeed, one review of the evidence available suggests that displacement (negative impact) and diffusion (positive impact) are almost equally likely. Of these, it seems temporal and target displacement are the most common forms, whereas spatial diffusion was the most common form, followed by target diffusion.

We must finish this discussion by acknowledging that the issues raised by situational prevention are not just technical or practical but are ones that raise ethical questions. Critics have argued, for example, that a prevention orientation helps maintain the status quo and diverts attention from the need for social reform; tends to protect the interests of the powerful against the relatively powerless; and encourages greater social exclusion via the targeting of particular groups and places. As early as 1961 the renowned campaigner and journalist, Jane Jacobs, made the important observation that: 'The well-used city street is apt to be a safe street. A deserted city street is apt to be unsafe.' She counselled against the development of a fortress mentality, and instead argued for the importance of those forms of everyday social interaction and surveillance we came across in Chapter 7 when discussing informal social control, which she suggested are the basis for a well-functioning urban community.

The focus on prevention

For much of the 20th century criminology was broadly optimistic in outlook, assuming that some mixture of general improvements in social conditions, together with developing knowledge about crime and criminality, would lead to diminishing crime levels. However, the early post-war decades, as we saw in Chapter 5, were characterized by sizeable and sustained rises in crime. Against this backdrop, optimism about the potential of reform and rehabilitative interventions began to decline. The growing pessimism that surrounded the efficacy of social interventions in this period was arguably largely misplaced, and has had significant negative consequences for both the politics of crime control and for investment in reformative efforts. It was in such circumstances, however, that what David Garland referred to as 'the new criminologies of everyday life' emerged. These opportunity-focused, SCP initiatives are undoubtedly criminology's most influential practical contribution to crime control in recent times. As with so much of criminology, a great deal of work in this area remains in its relative infancy, and rigorous research evidence is not nearly as plentiful as one might wish. Nevertheless, there are good grounds to believe that careful attention to what Marcus Felson referred to as the 'chemistry of crime' holds considerable potential for significant gains in crime reduction in the future.

Chapter 9
Where next for criminology?

In this Very Short Introduction to criminology, I have focused on a number of fundamental issues. What is crime? How much crime is there and how do we know? How might we explain long-term trends in crime? Who commits crime; and when and why do they stop? And how do we control or prevent crime? By this stage, I hope we might agree that these are important and interesting questions, and that criminology already has a few thoughtful answers to some of them. But what does the future hold?

By now you will also have become familiar with the fact that criminology has diverse disciplinary origins and influences. As I said at the outset, I think this is more of a strength than a weakness. There are multiple criminologies out there, often with their own label: cultural criminology, realist criminology, critical criminology, experimental criminology, and crime science among them. The labels generally indicate different theoretical predispositions, sometimes different methodological preferences or prejudices, as well as differing senses of what the key matters for criminology are thought to be.

To a degree the labels are also indicative of differing political positions—or, at least, positions that have differing political implications and likely consequences. In Chapter 8, for example, we noted the rise of rational choice-influenced, opportunity-focused approaches to SCP at a time when faith in more traditional, sociologically oriented criminological work was in decline. Differing bodies of work bring very different sets of priorities to the criminological enterprise—crime prevention focuses on events and situations; more sociological criminology on the social circumstances in which we might understand crime, criminal justice, and penal policy; and psychological criminology on offenders and their dispositions. Such contrasts are sufficient for some occasionally to argue that different approaches represent different paradigms.

Those of a more sociological bent have often been critical of the SCP-style approach for its absence of concern with what they take to be the deep-lying, structural bases of offending. SCP, they suggest, by avoiding a focus on underlying social problems—most obviously those linked to social inequality—avoids dealing with the fundamental causes of crime. At best, therefore, its practitioners are apolitical in their approach to their work; at worst, they are simply propping up the status quo, allowing social inequality and oppression to go unchallenged. By contrast, the defence of crime science and SCP is that it is hard-headed, practical, and effective. Moreover, it is suggested, it doesn't fall prey to an 'underdog sociology', an uncritical siding with the offender against an unfair and oppressive social system.

No doubt there are a number of potential observations one can draw from this. I simply wish to highlight two. The first is that the practice of criminology—however that term is understood—inevitably raises questions of politics and ethics. From the subject of study, the approach taken to research, to the objectives (explicit or implicit) of that research, criminological activity is inevitably political. Not only is it the case that the subject of criminology, crime, is a political phenomenon, often fought over by politicians for electoral gain, but the choices involved in how *to do* criminology necessarily reflect certain social values. The second straightforward observation is that criminology—as is true of all academic or scientific inquiry—takes place within particular historical and political conditions. The history of criminology itself can be, indeed must be, understood in part in political terms. That it emerged when it did, in the ways that it did, and has developed in the directions it has, reflects the nature of the times. The rise of SCP and the relative decline in the influence of a variety of sociological criminologies in part reflected the contemporary political mood—a period in which there was growing emphasis in all walks of life on individual choice and responsibility, and growing frustration with, and criticism of, welfarism. As I write—in the aftermath of Brexit and the election of President Trump, and with continuing economic turbulence—the political mood seems ever more febrile. No doubt social sciences, criminology included, will come to reflect upon this in varying and complex ways.

I began this book by drawing attention to the problematic core of criminology—the fact that part of its subject matter, crime, is a less straightforward notion than it might at first appear. So problematic that it has led some to call for an entirely different focus altogether—for example upon *harm* rather than crime. Although I am yet to be convinced that this solves the problem, it undeniably raises very significant issues for criminology, current and future. Undoubtedly the most important of these is criminology's continuing failure to pay sufficient attention to the crimes of the powerful.

This failure can be seen in a variety of ways. At its simplest, it is illustrated by criminology's continuing preoccupation with the common-or-garden crimes that fill the courts and subsequently the prisons of most developed societies, and its less concentrated focus on the crimes—where they are defined as crimes—or the harms caused by the wealthy and powerful. What criminologists have traditionally referred to as 'white-collar' and 'corporate' crimes account for a tiny proportion of criminological attention. That this is so reflects criminology's tendency too easily to accept 'crime' as defined by the state, rather than to think more broadly about its subject matter, including 'crimes' *by* the state. Certainly as far as its critics are concerned, much contemporary criminology is insufficiently questioning of the status quo.

Linked with this it can be argued that criminology continues to pay insufficient critical attention to the consequences of neoliberalism. Robert Reiner, one of the most consistent and thoughtful critics in this regard, has argued that important as the traditional concerns of criminology undoubtedly are, '*The* crimes of our times are those of capital'. Yet how much criminological scholarship, for example, was focused on the global financial crisis which began with problems in the US sub-prime mortgage system from late 2007 and the collapse of Lehman Brothers Bank in September 2008? Again, the answer is relatively little, and this reflects what was, until recently, contemporary criminology's somewhat limited interest in political economy. Fortunately, there are clear signs that this is beginning to change, particularly in respect of the comparative study of punishment. One can hope that criminology's immediate future will see a burgeoning of work that re-engages with issues of political economy and that it will focus as least as much on the misconduct of the powerful as it does on the crimes and misdemeanours of the powerless.

A criminology which does this will also need to pay more attention to global inequalities. For much of its history, criminology has been dominated by work from the English-speaking world and this book has been no exception to the largely Northern hemispheric, Anglo-American view of criminology's concerns—though by now it should be clear that this is far from being a homogenous body of work. In recent years a growing group of scholars have begun to develop a 'Southern' perspective, which seeks to broaden the criminological gaze or, as is argued, to 'de-colonize and democratize' it. The traditional Northern focus of criminology, they argue, has tended to neglect such phenomena as the impact of colonialism and the often very different histories and practices of policing, punishment, and dispute resolution that exist in other cultures, and a reorientation of criminology's concerns is consequently needed.

Criminology's concerns are already sizeable. They encompass matters of sociology, psychology, law, political science, economics, history, and biology to name a few. Its core questions range from the profoundly philosophical to the broadly practical. Its methods draw from both the social and the physical sciences. At heart, criminology's focus remains those forms of human conduct we treat as criminal or deviant, or which produce such harms intervention is argued to be necessary. Yet the swiftly changing nature of the world we inhabit poses huge challenges for criminologists. Globalization, the increasingly complex and transnational nature of economic power, the growing voluntary and forced movement of peoples across borders, the spreading influence and impact of the Internet and new communication technologies, the profound risks posed by environmental change—each and all of these raise huge questions for criminology. And they are questions we cannot afford to ignore. Rising to these challenges guarantees an exciting future for criminology.

References and further reading

General introductions to the field:

Adler, F. (2013) *Criminology*. Maidenhead: McGraw Hill.

Liebling, A., Maruna, S., and McAra, L. (eds) (2017) *Oxford Handbook of Criminology*. Oxford: Oxford University Press.

Newburn, T. (2017) *Criminology*. London: Routledge.

Reiner, R. (2016) *Crime*. Cambridge: Polity Press.

Tonry, M. (2013) *Oxford Handbook of Crime and Criminal Justice*. New York: Oxford University Press.

Chapter 1: Introducing criminology

Sources of quotations in this chapter:

'A philosopher produces ideas...': Marx and Engels, *Collected Works*, vol. 30; quoted also in Wheen, F. (1999) *Karl Marx*. London: Fourth Estate, pp. 308–9.

'[Criminology] has no distinct theoretical object...', Garland, D. (2011) Criminology's place in the academic field, in Bosworth, M. and Hoyle, C. (eds), *What is Criminology?* Oxford: Oxford University Press.

On the history and place of criminology:

Beirne, P. (1993) *Inventing Criminology*. London: SUNY Press.

Bosworth, M. and Hoyle, C. (eds) (2011) *What is Criminology?* Oxford: Oxford University Press.

Garland, D. (1985) The criminal and his science: a critical account of the formation of criminology at the end of the nineteenth century, *British Journal of Criminology* 25: 109–37.

Garland, D. (2002) Of crimes and criminals: the development of criminology in Britain, in Maguire, M., Morgan, R. and Reiner, R. (eds), *The Oxford Handbook of Criminology*. Oxford: Oxford University Press.

Rafter, N. (ed.) (2009) *Origins of Criminology: Readings from the Nineteenth Century*. London: Routledge.

Chapter 2: What is crime?

Sources of quotations in this chapter:

'A husband cannot be guilty of rape...': Pateman, C. (1980) Women and consent, *Political Theory* 8/2: 149–68.

Times of India, 'Why isn't marital rape a crime in India?', 9 September, <http://timesofindia.indiatimes.com/life-style/relationships/love-sex/Why-isnt-marital-rape-a-criminal-offence-in-India/articleshow/54223996.cms> (accessed 9 February 2017).

United Nations General Assembly (2015) Report of the Special Rapporteur on Freedom of Religion or Belief, 23 December, UN: A/HRC/31/18.

On violence against women:

United Nations General Assembly (2006) In-depth study of all forms of violence against women, <https://documents-dds-ny.un.org/doc/UNDOC/GEN/N06/419/74/PDF/N0641974.pdf?OpenElement>.

Randall, M. and Venkatesh, V. (2006) Symposium on the international legal obligation to criminalize marital rape: criminalizing sexual violence against women in intimate relationships: State obligations under human rights law, *American Journal of International Law Unbound*, January.

On the James Bulger and Silje Redergard cases:

Green, D.A. (2008) *When Children Kill Children*. Oxford: Clarendon Press

On stop and frisk in the US and other jurisdictions:

New York Civil Liberties Union: <http://www.nyclu.org/content/stop-and-frisk-data>.

Gelman, A., Fagan, J., and Kiss, A. (2012) An analysis of New York City Police Department's 'stop and frisk' policy in the context of claims of racial bias, *Journal of the American Statistical Association*, 102/479: 813–23.

Bowling, B. and Phillips, C. (2007) Disporportionate and discriminatory: reviewing the evidence on police stop and search, *Modern Law Review*, 70/6: 936–61.

On indigenous imprisonment in Australia:

Weatherburn, D. (2014) Arresting Incarceration: Pathways Out of Indigenous Imprisonment. Canberra: Australian Institute of Aboriginal and Torres Strait Islander Studies.

Weatherburn, D. and Ramsay, S. (2016) What is causing the growth in indigenous imprisonment in New South Wales? Sydney: NSW Bureau of Crime Statistics and Research, Issue paper no.118, August.

On (corporate) crime and harm:

Tombs, S. and Whyte, D. (2015) *The Corporate Criminal*. London: Routledge.

Hillyard, P. and Tombs, S. (2007) From 'crime' to 'social harm', *Crime, Law and Social Change*, 48/1–2: 9–25.

Chapter 3: Who commits crime?

On criminal careers and patterns of offending:

Wolfgang, M.E., Figlio, R.M., and Sellin, T. (1972) *Delinquency in a Birth Cohort*. Chicago: University of Chicago Press.

Loeber, R., Farrington, D.P., Stouthamer-Loeber, M, and White, H.R. (2008) *Violence and Serious Theft: Development and Prediction from Childhood to Adulthood*. New York: Routledge.

Prime, J., White, S., Liriano, S., and Patel, K. (2001) Criminal careers of those born between 1953 and 1978. Statistical Bulletin 4/01. London: Home Office.

Clancy, A., Hough, M., Aust, C., and Kershaw, C. (2001) *Crime, Policing and Justice: The Experience of Ethnic Minorities. Findings from the 2000 British Crime Survey*. London: Home Office.

Comparing different data sources:

Jolliffe, D. and Farrington, D.P. (2014) Self-reported offending: Reliability and validity, in Bruinsma, G. and Weisburd, D. (eds), *Encyclopedia of Criminology and Criminal Justice*. New York: Springer-Verlag.

Piquero, A.R., Schubert, C., and Brame, R. (2014) Comparing official and self-report records of offending across gender and race/ethnicity in a longitudinal study of serious youthful offenders, *Journal of Research in Crime and Delinquency*, 51: 526–56.

Farrington, D.P., Auty, K.M., Coid, J.W., and Turner, R.E. (2013) Self-reported and official offending from age 10 to age 56, *European Journal of Criminal Policy and Research*, 19: 135–51.

Offending, gender, and ethnicity:

Moffitt, T.E., Caspi, M., Rutter, P., and Silva, A. (2001) *Sex Differences in Antisocial Behaviour: Conduct Disorder, Delinquency and Violence in the Dunedin Longitudinal Study*. Cambridge: Cambridge University Press.

Piquero, A.R. and Brame, R.W. (2008) Assessing the race-crime and ethnicity-crime relationship in a sample of serious adolescent delinquents, *Crime and Delinquency*, 54/3: 390–422.

Sampson, R.J., Morenoff, J.D., and Raudenbush, S.W. (2005) Social anatomy of racial and ethnic disparities in violence, *American Journal of Public Health*, 95: 224–32.

White-collar offending:

Braithwaite, J. (1979). *Inequality, Crime and Public Policy*. London: Routledge.

Tombs, S. and Whyte, D. (2015) Introduction to the special issue on 'Crimes of the powerful', *Howard Journal*, 54/1: 1–7.

Klenowski, P.M. and Dodson, K.D. (2016) Who commits white-collar crime, and what do we know about them?, in Van Slyke, S.R., Benson, M.L., and Cullen, F.T. (eds), *The Oxford Handook of White Collar Crime*. New York: Oxford University Press.

Cohen, M.A. (2016) The costs of white collar crime, in Van Slyke, S., Benson, M.L., and Cullen, F.T. (eds), *Oxford Handbook of White Collar Crime*. New York: Oxford University Press.

Costs of crime:

Anderson, D.A. (2012) The cost of crime, *Foundations and Trends in Microeconomics*, 7: 209–65.

Distribution of offending:

'adult antisocial behaviour virtually requires childhood antisocial behaviour': Robins, L.N. (1978) Sturdy childhood predictors of adult antisocial behaviour: replications from longitudinal studies, *Psychological Medicine*, 8: 611–22, at p. 611.

Farrington, D. and West, D. (1993) Criminal, penal and life histories of chronic offenders: risk and protective factors and early identification, *Criminal Behaviour and Mental Health*, 3: 492–523.

Farrington, D. (2010) Life-course and developmental theories in criminology, in McLaughlin, E. and Newburn, T. (eds), *Sage Handbook of Criminological Theory*. London: Sage.

Moffitt, T.E. (1993) Adolescence-limited and life-course-persistent antisocial behavior: a developmental taxonomy, *Psychological Review*, 100/4: 674–701.

Raine, A. (2013) *The Anatomy of Violence: The Biological Roots of Crime*. London: Penguin.

Raine, A. (2002) Biosocial studies of antisocial and violent behaviour in children and adults: a review, *Journal of Abnormal Child Psychology*, 30/4: 311–26.

'You cannot pin the blame on poverty...': Raine, A. (2013) *The Anatomy of Violence: The Biological Roots of Crime*. London: Allen Lane.

Desistance:

Sampson, R.J. and Laub, J. (2005) A life-course view of the development of crime, *Annals of the American Academy of Political and Social Science*, 602: 12–45.

Maruna, S. (2001) *Making Good: How Ex-Convicts Reform and Rebuild their Lives*. Washington DC: American Psychological Association.

Chapter 4: How do we measure crime?

On measures of crime:

Tonry, M. and Farrington, D. (2005) *Crime and Punishment in Western Countries 1980–1999*. Chicago: University of Chicago Press.

Langton, L. (2012) *Victimizations not reported to the police, 2006–2010*. US Department of Justice Special Report, NCJ 238536.

Donald Cressey, 'police have an obligation to protect the reputation of their cities...', quoted in: Wolfgang, M.E. (1962–3) Uniform crime reports: a critical appraisal, *University of Pennsylvania Law Review*, 111: 708.

Xu, J. (2017) Legitimization imperative: the production of crime statistics in Guangzhou, China, *British Journal of Criminology*, 58/1: 155–76.

In Australia:
Ombudsman Victoria (2009) *Crime Statistics and Police Numbers*, Session 2006-09 P.P. No. 173, March.

In England and Wales:
Public Administration Committee (2014) *Caught red-handed: why we can't count on police recorded crime statistics*, Thirteenth Report.

Measuring violence against women:
Kruttschnitt, C., Kalsbeek, W.D., and House, C.C. (eds) (2014) *Panel on Measuring Rape and Sexual Assault in Bureau of Justice Statistics Household Surveys*. London: National Academies Press.
Committee on National Statistics: <http://sites.nationalacademies.org>.
Division on Behavioral and Social Sciences and Education, National Research Council, Washington DC, <http://sites.nationalacademies.org/DBASSE/index.htm>.
Lauritsen, J.L., Gatewood Owens, J., Planty, M., Rand, M.R., and Truman, J.L. (2012) *Methods for Counting High-Frequency Repeat Victimizations in the National Crime Victimization Survey*, NCJ 237308. Washington DC: US Department of Justice.
Walby, S. and Myhill, A. (2001) New methodologies in researching violence against women, *British Journal of Criminology*, 41/3: 502–22.
Walby, S., Towers, J., and Francis, B. (2016) Is violence increasing or decreasing? A new methodology to measure repeat attacks making visible the significance of gender and domestic relations, *British Journal of Criminology*, 56/6: 1203–34.

Chapter 5: Understanding recent trends in crime

General overview:
Garland, D. (2001) *The Culture of Control*. Oxford: Oxford University Press.

On the impact of insurance:
Moss, E. (2011) Burglary insurance and the culture of fear in Britain, c. 1889–1939, *Historical Journal*, 54/4: 1039–64.

Michelbacher, G.L. and Carr, F.H. (undated) Burglary, theft and robbery insurance, <https://www.casact.org/pubs/proceed/proceed24/24033.pdf>.

Routine activities:
Cohen, L. and Felson, M. (1979) Social change and crime rate trends: a routine activities approach, *American Sociological Review*, 44/3: 588–608.

The civilizing process and crime:
Elias, N. (1978) *The Civilizing Process.* Oxford: Blackwell.
Pinker, S. (2011) *The Better Angels of our Nature.* London: Penguin.
Eisner, M. (2001) Modernization, self-control and lethal violence: the long-term dynamics of European homicide rates in theoretical perspective, *British Journal of Criminology*, 41/4: 618–38.

The 'underclass' and crime:
Murray, C.A. (1990) *The Emerging British Underclass.* London: Institute of Economic Affairs.
Lister, R. (1996) *Charles Murray and the Underclass: The Developing Debate.* London: Institute for Economic Affairs.

Chapter 6: Understanding the crime drop

General overview:
Farrell, G., Tilley, N., and Tseloni, A. (2014) Why the crime drop?, in Tonry, M. (ed.), *Crime and Justice*, 43: 421–89.
Tonry, M. (2014) Why crime rates are falling throughout the Western world, in Tonry, M. (ed.), *Crime and Justice*, 43: 1–62.
Baumer, E.P. and Wolff, K.T. (2014) Evaluating contemporary crime drop(s) in America, New York City, and many other places, *Justice Quarterly*, 31/1: 41–74.
Roeder, O., Eisen, L-B., and Bowling, J. (2015) *What Caused the Crime Decline?* New York: Brennan Center for Justice, New York University.
Levitt, S.D. (2004) Understanding why crime fell in the 1990s: four factors that explain the decline and six that do not, *Journal of Economic Perspectives*, 18/1: 163–90.
Zimring, F. (2007) *The Great American Crime Decline.* New York: Oxford University Press.

Political economy:

Reiner, R. (2016) *Crime*. Cambridge: Polity Press.

Lynch, M.J. (2012) Re-examining political economy and crime and explaining the crime drop, *Journal of Crime and Justice*, 36/2: 248–62.

Deterrence and recidivism:

Tonry, M. (2008) Learning from the limitations of deterrence research, *Crime and Justice*, 37/1: 279–311.

Nagin, D. (2013) Deterrence in the twenty-first century, *Crime and Justice*, 42/1: 199–263.

Durose, M.R., Snyder, H.N., and Cooper, A.D. (2014) Multistate criminal history patterns of prisoners released in 30 states, U.S. Department of Justice, NCJ 248942.

Weatherburn, D. (2010) The effect of imprisonment on adult reoffending, *Crime and Justice Bulletin*, New South Wales: Bureau of Crime Statistics and Research.

Incapacitation:

Zimring, F. and Hawkins, G. (1995) *Incapacitation: Penal Confinement and the Restraint of Crime*. New York: Oxford University Press.

Spelman, W. (2000) The limited importance of prison expansion, in Blumstein, A. (ed.), *The Crime Drop in America*. New York: Cambridge University Press.

Skarbek, D. (2014) *The Social Order of the Underworld*. Oxford: Oxford University Press.

Policing:

Braga, A.A. (2014) The effects of hot spots policing on crime: an updated systematic review and meta-analysis, *Justice Quarterly*, 31/4: 633–63.

Zimring, F. (2012) *The City that Became Safe: New York's Lessons for Urban Crime and Its Control*. New York: Oxford University Press.

Security hypothesis:

Martinson, R. (1974) What works? Questions and answers about prison reform, *The Public Interest*, 35: 22–54.

Clarke, R.V.G. and Newman, G. (2006) *Outsmarting the Terrorists*. Westport, CT: Praeger.

Farrell, G. (2011) The crime drop and the security hypothesis, *Journal of Research in Crime and Delinquency*, 48/2: 147–75.

Abortion law reform:

Donohue, J.J. and Levitt, S.D. (2001) The impact of legalized abortion on crime, *Quarterly Journal of Economics*, 116/2: 379–420.

Lead in petrol:

Nevin, R. (2000) How lead exposure relates to temporal changes in I.Q., violent crime and unwed pregnancy, *Environmental Research*, 83: 1–22.

Nevin, R. (2007) Understanding international crime trends: the legacy of preschool lead exposure, *Environmental Research*, 104: 315–36.

Weatherburn, D., Halstead, I., and Ramsay, S. (2016) The great (Australian) property crime decline, *Australian Journal of Social Issues*, 15/3: 257–78.

Chapter 7: How do we control crime?

Informal social control:

Tittle, C. (1980) *Sanctions and Social Deviance*. New York: Praeger.

Goffman, E. (1983) The interaction order, American Sociological Assocation, 1982 Presidential Address, *American Sociological Review*, 48/1: 1–17.

Toby, J. (1957) Social disorganization and a stake in conformity: complementary factors in the predatory behavior of hoodlums, *Journal of Criminology, Criminal Law and Police Science*, 48: 12–17.

Shapland, J. and Vagg, J. (1988) *Policing by the Public*. London: Routledge.

Control theory:

Hirschi, T. (1969) *Causes of Delinquency*. Berkeley, CA: University of California Press.

Gottfredson, M. and Hirschi, T. (1990) *A General Theory of Crime*. Stanford: Stanford University Press.

Pasternoster, R. and Bachman, R. (2010) Control theories, in McLaughlin, E. and Newburn, T. (eds), *The Sage Handbook of Criminological Theory*. London: Sage.

Age-graded theory:

Sampson, R. and Laub, J.H. (1993) *Crime in the Making: Pathways and Turning Points through Life*. Cambridge, MA: Harvard University Press.

Laub, J.H. and Sampson, R.J. (2003) *Shared Beginnings, Divergent Lives: Delinquent Boys at Age 70*. Cambridge, MA: Harvard University Press.

Sampson, R.J., Raudenbush, S.W., and Earls, F. (1997) Neighbourhoods and violent crime: a multilevel study of collective efficacy, *Science*, 277/5328: 918–24.

Chapter 8: How do we prevent crime?

'A calm and dispassionate recognition...': Winston Churchill: *Hansard Parliamentary Debates*, HC Deb, 20 July 1910 vol. 19, *c*.1354.

On the 'rehabilitative ideal':
Garland, D. (1987) *Punishment and Welfare*. London: Gower.

Defensible space/CPED:
Newman, O. (1972) *Defensible Space*. New York: Collier.
Jeffery, C. Ray. (1971) *Crime Prevention through Environmental Design*. London: Sage.

Social crime prevention:
High/Scope Perry Pre-School Project: <https://highscope.org/perrypreschoolstudy>.
Parks, G. (2000) The High/Scope Perry Pre-School Project, U.S. Department of Justice *Office of Juvenile Justice and Delinquency Prevention*, October Bulletin.

Rational choice:
Clarke, R. and Cornish, D. (2001) Rational choice, in Paternoster, R. and Bachman, R. (eds), *Explaining Criminals and Crime*. Los Angeles: Roxbury.
Cornish, R. and Clarke, R. (2014) *The Reasoning Criminal*. London: Transaction.

Impact of CCTV:
Welsh, B.C. and Farrington, D.P. (2009) Public-area CCTV and crime prevention: an updated systematic review and meta-analysis, *Justice Quarterly*, 26/4: 716–45.

New York crime decline:

Kelling, G. and Bratton, W. (1998) Declining crime rates: insiders' views of the New York City story, *Journal of Criminal Law and Criminology*, 88/4: 1217–31.

Harcourt, B. (2001) *Illusion of Order.* Cambridge, MA: Harvard University Press.

Techniques of neutralization:

Sykes, G. and Matza, D. (1957) Techniques of neutralization: a theory of delinquency, *American Sociological Review*, 22/6: 664.

Violence reduction and prevention in prison:

Wortley, R. and Summers, L. (2005) Reducing prison disorder through situational prevention: the Glen Parva experience, in Smith, M.J. and Tilley, N. (eds), *Crime Science: New Approaches to Preventing and Detecting Crime.* Cullompton: Willan Publishing.

Repeat victimization:

Farrell, G., Tseloni, A., and Pease, K., 2005. Repeat victimization in the ICVS and the NCVS, *Crime Prevention and Community Safety: An International Journal*, 7/3: 7–18.

Farrell, G., Phillips, C., and Pease, K. (1995) Like taking candy: why does repeat victimization occur? *British Journal of Criminology*, 35/3: 384–99.

Gas suicide:

Clarke, R.V. and Mayhew, P. (1988) The British Gas suicide story and its criminological implications, *Crime and Justice*, vol. 10. Chicago: University of Chicago Press.

Displacement and diffusion of crime:

Weisburd, D. et al. (2006) Does crime just move around the corner? *Criminology*, 44/3: 549–91.

Weisburd, D., Wyckoff, L.A., Ready, J., Eck, J.E., Hinkle, J.C., and Gajewski, F. (2006) Does crime just move around the corner? A controlled study of spatial displacement and diffusion of crime control benefits, *Criminology*, 44: 549–92.

Guerette, R.T. and Bowers, K.J. (2009) Assessing the extent of crime displacement and diffusion of benefits: a review of situational crime prevention evaluations, *Criminology*, 47/4: 1331–68.

The ethics of situational prevention:

Von Hirsch, A., Garland, D., and Wakefield, A. (eds) (2004) *Ethical and Social Perspectives on Situational Crime Prevention.* Oxford: Hart.

'The well-used city street...' Jacobs, J. (1992) *The Death and Life of Great American Cities.* New York: Pantheon, p. 34.

Chapter 9: Where next for criminology?

'*The* crimes of our times are those of capital':

Reiner, R. (2016) *Crime.* London: Polity Press.

A nice collection of essays offering a variety of perspectives on criminology's past, present, and future can be found in:

Bosworth, M. and Hoyle, C. (2011) *What is Criminology?* Oxford: Oxford University Press.

Index

Index

FORENSIC
PSYCHOLOGY
A Very Short Introduction
David Canter

Lie detection, offender profiling, jury selection, insanity in
the law, predicting the risk of re-offending, the minds of serial
killers and many other topics that fill news and fiction are all
aspects of the rapidly developing area of scientific psychology
broadly known as Forensic Psychology. *Forensic Psychology:
A Very Short Introduction* discusses all the aspects of psychology
that are relevant to the legal and criminal process as a whole.
It includes explanations of criminal behaviour and criminality,
including the role of mental disorder in crime, and discusses
how forensic psychology contributes to helping investigate
the crime and catching the perpetrators.

www.oup.com/vsi

FORENSIC SCIENCE
A Very Short Introduction
Jim Fraser

In this Very Short Introduction, Jim Fraser introduces the concept of forensic science and explains how it is used in the investigation of crime. He begins at the crime scene itself, explaining the principles and processes of crime scene management. He explores how forensic scientists work; from the reconstruction of events to laboratory examinations. He considers the techniques they use, such as fingerprinting, and goes on to highlight the immense impact DNA profiling has had. Providing examples from forensic science cases in the UK, US, and other countries, he considers the techniques and challenges faced around the world.

> An admirable alternative to the 'CSI' science fiction juggernaut...Fascinating.
>
> **William Darragh, Fortean Times**

www.oup.com/vsi

LAW
A Very Short Introduction
Raymond Wacks

Law underlies our society - it protects our rights, imposes duties on each of us, and establishes a framework for the conduct of almost every social, political, and economic activity. The punishment of crime, compensation of the injured, and the enforcement of contracts are merely some of the tasks of a modern legal system. It also strives to achieve justice, promote freedom, and protect our security. This *Very Short Introduction* provides a clear, jargon-free account of modern legal systems, explaining how the law works both in the Western tradition and around the world.

www.oup.com/vsi